?

I'm Glad You Asked That !

Questions From Parishioners

Fr. John Noone

and

Ron Young

I'm Glad You Asked That!

Questions From Parishioners

Throughout this discussion, scripture quotations are taken from either the New International Version (NIV), (copyright 1973, 1978, 1984 by International Bible Society, used by permission of Zondervan Bible Publishers), or the King James Version (KJV), (no copyright) of the Holy Bible rather than from approved Catholic translations. This is not because there is any fault in the Catholic translation, but because the NIV and the KJV are among the most popular Protestant translations, and whenever possible we should point out to our separated brothers and sisters that their translations of the Holy Bible support the doctrines of the Catholic Church.

Quotations taken from an approved Catholic translation are from the Revised Standard Version, Catholic Edition (RSV-CE) (New Testament copyright 1965 and Old Testament copyright 1966 by Division of Christian Education of the National Council of the Churches of Christ in the United States of America).

https://frjohnnoonesbooks.wordpress.com/

ISBN 978-1-7351946-7-7

Credit: https://www.wpclipart.com/religion_mythology/new_testament/Jesus/sermon_on_the_mount_BW.png.html

TABLE OF CONTENTS

INTRODUCTION

Parishioners were requested to submit questions that they had been asked about their faith or questions that they themselves had about their faith. The purpose of these questions was not to write a book, but to enable us to address these questions during the Sunday homilies in order to provide answers and raise the consciousness of the parish about things Catholic.

As it turned out, the questions were so good and covered such a wide variety of topics that we felt that it would be most convenient to put many of the questions and answers into a booklet which everyone could use as a reference. We have all been called by Jesus to evangelize, but many today don't know how to start; or believe that they don't have the proper background. The easiest way to evangelize is to LIVE YOUR FAITH every day and when questioned, provide an answer. Saint Peter said,

> "Always be prepared to make a defense to any one who calls you to account for the hope that is in you, yet do it with gentleness and reverence; and keep your conscience clear, so that, when you are abused, those who revile your good behavior in Christ may be put to shame." (1 Peter 3:15-16 RSV-CE).

Jesus also said,

> "So, every one who acknowledges me before men, I also will acknowledge before my Father who is in heaven; but whoever denies me before men, I also will deny before my Father who is in heaven." (Matthew 10:32-33 RSV-CE).

Many of the more common questions one may be asked are addressed in this booklet. If you are asked a question which is not addressed, or you don't have an immediate answer, don't make one up. Instead say, "I don't know right now but I'll find out and get back with you," then look it up or contact your priest. In any case, you can always say, "I'm Glad You Asked That!", and begin to share your faith.

Yours in Christ,
Fr. John Noone
Ron Young

Ron Young, a convert to Catholicism and having a wealth of knowledge about the Bible and the Church, researched these subjects thoroughly.

SIN

Q. My Non-Catholic friends think we are crazy to separate sins into venial and mortal. How can I explain the difference to them?

A. The easiest way is to refer them to 1 John 5:16-17 in their Bible:

> "If anyone sees his brother commit a sin that does not lead to death, he should pray, and God will give him life. I refer to those whose sin does not lead to death. There is a sin that leads to death. [This is the sin which Catholics call mortal sin.] I am not saying you should pray about that. All wrongdoing is sin, and there is sin that does not lead to death." [This is the sin which Catholics call venial sin.] (1 John 5:16-17 NIV).

Simply put, all sin is an offense against God because it sets itself against God's love for us and turns our hearts away from Him. Mortal sin is a grave violation of God's law and destroys charity in the heart of man. Mortal sin is not capable of being forgiven through any power within the soul itself. A special intervention by God is required (much like the human body which, once it dies, can only be resurrected by God). This is why Catholics have the

Sacrament of Reconciliation (penance/confession); so that God can again become sacramentally present and active in our lives. For a sin to be mortal, three conditions must all be met:

1. The object must be a grave matter,
2. It must be committed with full knowledge,
3. And it must be committed with deliberate consent.

Venial sin allows charity to subsist in the soul, even though it offends and wounds the soul. The term "venial" comes from the Latin word "venia" which means pardon. This term is applied to less than mortal sin because the soul has a vital principle that allows a cure from within (much like a diseased or sick body which fights off the infection and recovers).

Recommended Reading:

Catechism of the Catholic Church, Libreria Editrice Vaticana, 1994, paras. 1854-1864.

Hardon, John A., S.J., *The Catholic Catechism*, Doubleday, New York, NY, 1981, pp. 183-185.

Q. What is the unforgivable sin?

A. Luke 12:10 NIV says:

> "And everyone who speaks a word against the Son of Man will be forgiven, but anyone who blasphemes against the Holy Spirit will not be forgiven." (See also Matthew 12:32 and Mark 3:29.)

Blasphemy against the Holy Spirit is to reject His grace. Not allowing the Holy Spirit to work in our lives is blasphemy. It is saying, "I know more than God does about what is right for me." Thus, takes away the principle which makes it possible to ask for forgiveness.

This manifests itself in four ways:

1. Despair concerning the possibility of salvation;
2. Presumption of God's mercy and forgiveness;
3. Denial of the truths of faith; and
4. Final impenitence and refusal to turn to God.

Sins against the Holy Spirit are the gravest of sins, because they reject the dignity of the One (Jesus) sent by the Father to sanctify us and restore us to full union with Him. Belief that if anyone fails to be open to the workings of the Holy Spirit in their lives, even once, automatically condemns them to Hell forever, is not the teaching of this passage in Holy Scripture. This passage addresses the condition of the soul at the moment of death. Prior to that moment, every person has the opportunity to turn to God, to have their sins forgiven, and be welcomed home like the prodigal son (Luke 15:11-32).

<u>Recommended Reading:</u>

Catechism of the Catholic Church, Libreria Editrice Vaticana, 1994, para 1864.

Stravinskas, Rev. Peter M. J., *Our Sunday Visitor Catholic Encyclopedia,* Our Sunday Visitor, Huntington, IN 46750, 1991, p. 481.

*To Sin Is to Die, Booklet #49,*1967, Catholic Information Service, Knights of Columbus, P.O. Box 1971, New Haven CT 06521.

Q. Is it a mortal sin to miss Mass on Sundays?

A. The 3rd Commandment tells us to keep the Lord's Day holy. In Old Testament times, God's people stopped working and gathered together for worship on the Sabbath, which was Saturday. However, the early Christians rested and came together to rejoice on Sunday because Jesus, Our Lord and Savior, rose from the dead, on Easter Sunday morning. Also, the Holy Spirit came on the Apostles and Mary on Sunday. Sunday is not only a day of worship but a day of joy and family closeness.

Now as to whether it is a mortal sin or not, the three conditions for determining whether or not a sin is mortal were described under the question on mortal and venial sin.

1. There must be a grave matter: It is a grave matter to miss Mass on Sunday.
2. Full Knowledge: If we have full knowledge that it is a sinful matter to violate one of the Ten Commandments because it violates God's law, then the second condition is met.
3. Full consent of the will: Suppose we realize that the 3rd Commandment requires us to gather together to worship, and we know that it is a grave sinful matter to violate the Commandments, but the car won't start, and there is no

other way to get to Mass. Then, the third condition has not been met, and there is no sin. If, however, we simply miss Mass because there is something else that we would rather be doing (like playing golf, going to the beach, etc.) then a deliberate act has taken place, and a mortal sin has been committed. It's like saying, "I don't love God enough to spend some of my time with Him."

Recommended Reading:

Catechism of the Catholic Church, Libreria Editrice Vaticana, 1994, paras. 1857-1861.

Remember The Sabbath …Keep It Holy, Booklet #36, 1967, Catholic Information Service, Knights of Columbus, P.O. Box 1971, New Haven CT 06521.

Q. Is masturbation a mortal sin? If it is, why?

A. First, we must understand that our sexual organs are good and beautiful because they were given to us by God for the most noble purpose of continuing the human race. Genesis 1:27-28 NIV says:

> "So, God created mankind in his own image, in the image of God he created them; male and female he created them. God blessed them and said to them. 'Be fruitful and increase in number; fill the earth and subdue it."

Our sexual organs were given to us by God; his for her and hers for him so that this command can be fulfilled.

Second, the sex act in marriage is also good and beautiful because of its twofold God-given purpose:

1. For the generation of children
2. And as an expression of true mutual love between the spouses.

God performed the initial act of creation when He formed Adam and took the woman from his side. In the sex act in marriage, the couple is complying with God's command and is in essence performing an act of re-creation; with God's help, they are creating a new life.

Masturbation is the deliberate stimulation of the sex organ in order to derive sexual pleasure. As such, it is an act of recreation rather than of re-creation and is ordered toward self rather than toward God. The 6th Commandment is, "You shall not commit adultery (Exodus 20:14 and Deuteronomy 5:18)", and this prohibits any sexual activity except with one's lifelong partner in the Sacrament of Matrimony. Even if one is not married, the teaching of the Catholic Church has always been that the 6th Commandment encompasses all sexual activity. After all, Jesus said that the greatest commandment was that we shall, "Love the Lord your God with all your heart and with all your soul and with all your mind and with all your strength (Mark 12:30, NIV)", and self-centered recreational sexual activity violates this command.

Whether masturbation is a mortal or venial sin depends upon the conditions for a sin to be mortal which were given in the answer to the question on mortal and venial sin. If one knows that it is a grave sin and why, then, it is a mortal sin.

Recommended Reading:

Catechism of the Catholic Church, Libreria Editrice Vaticana, 1994, para. 2352.

Hardon, John A., S.J., *The Catholic Catechism*, Doubleday, New York, NY, 12020, 1981, pp. 354-356.

Drummey, James J., *Catholic Replies*, C. R. Publications, Norwood, MA 02062, 1995, pp. 407-410.

Q. If we sin, can we bless ourselves with holy water and take Communion or do we have to go to Confession?

A: All mortal sins require the sacramental presence of God in our lives to be restored. For this reason, all mortal sins require the Sacrament of Reconciliation (penance/confession) in order to obtain absolution. One must not be in a state of mortal sin and receive the Eucharist because to do so would constitute another mortal sin. In the case of venial sins, blessing oneself with holy water is not sufficient to remove the stain of the sin and receive the Eucharist, but it is a start. A sincere act of contrition and a sincere participation in the Penitential Rite of the Mass will absolve venial sins and the Eucharist can be received.

Recommended Reading:

Stravinskas, Peter M. J., *The Catholic Answer Book*, Our Sunday Visitor, Huntington, IN, 1990, p. 31.

Q. Is it a sin to drink alcohol?
Q. Is it a sin to get drunk?

A. Nowhere in the Bible is the use of alcoholic beverages prohibited. If it were sinful, would Jesus have changed water into wine at Cana (John 2: 1-11)? Jesus drank wine and was falsely accused of being a drunkard (Matthew 11:19). The drinking of alcoholic beverages is nothing more than making use of what God has provided and is not a sinful act. In fact, the Bible says:

> "He causeth the grass to grow for the cattle, and herb for the service of man: that he may bring forth food out of the earth; And wine that maketh glad the heart of man, and oil to make his face to shine, and bread which strengtheneth man's heart." (Psalm 104:14-15 KJV).

> "Drink no longer water, but use a little wine for thy stomach's sake and thine often infirmities." (1 Timothy 5:23 KJV).

Notice that Holy Scripture says, "a little wine", not copious quantities. Use of any alcoholic beverage to the point of becoming intoxicated is a misuse of God's gift and is a sinful act. Throughout the Bible there is a clear distinction made between the use of alcohol and the abuse of alcohol (for example; Ephesians 5:18 and Proverbs 20:1).

Recommended Reading:

Catechism of the Catholic Church, Libreria Editrice Vaticana, 1994, para. 2290.

Mbukanma, Rev. Jude O., *Is it in the Bible?*, Scripture Keys Ministries Australia, Broadford, Victoria, Australia, 1987, pp. 59-66.

Q. Is it a sin to gamble?

A. Matthias was chosen by lot as the Apostle to replace Judas Iscariot (Acts 1:26). In Leviticus 16:8, Aaron casts lots to determine which goat is to be sacrificed for the people and which is to be released into the desert. In Joshua 18:10, Joshua casts lots to determine what portion of the promised land each tribe is to receive. Casting lots is a form of gambling. If the Apostles did it and recorded it in Holy Scripture without condemning it, it must not be a sinful act. All this said, any time someone gambles away something to the detriment of their attention to God, to themselves, or to their family, then it becomes a sinful act.

Recommended Reading:

Catechism of the Catholic Church, Libreria Editrice Vaticana, 1994, para. 2413.

Q. Is it wrong to "shop around" for a priest to let you use birth control?

A. From the way the question is worded it is obvious that this person is aware that contraception is a serious matter and has full knowledge that it is a sinful act, so this person looking for a loophole which will allow them to escape the blame of giving full consent (so, the three conditions for determining mortal sin are fulfilled: a grave matter, full knowledge, and willful consent). There are no loopholes. Any sinful act is always a sinful act, even if one has "permission" to do it. No priest (or bishop) can legitimately give "permission" to engage in any sinful act.

Q. Is it a mortal sin to receive Communion without believing that it is truly the Body, Blood, Soul and Divinity of Christ?

A. The National Conference of Catholic Bishops has set up guidelines which are printed in every missalette: "Catholics fully participate in the celebration of the Eucharist when they receive Holy Communion in fulfillment of Christ's command to eat His Body and drink His Blood. In order to be properly disposed to receive Communion, communicants should not be conscious of grave sin, have fasted for one hour, and seek to live in charity and love with their neighbors. A person conscious of grave sin must first be reconciled with God and the Church through the Sacrament of Penance. A frequent reception of the Sacrament of Penance is encouraged for all."

The Catholic belief is that Holy Communion is in fact the Body, Blood, Soul and Divinity of Our Lord Jesus Christ. This belief will be more thoroughly discussed in the chapter on the Sacrament of the Eucharist. As to whether receiving Holy Communion without believing this, we look to what Saint Paul says as he writes in 1 Corinthians 11:23-29 KJV:

> "For I have received of the Lord that which also I delivered unto you, that the Lord Jesus the same night in which he was betrayed took bread: And when he had given thanks, he brake it, and said, Take, eat: this is my body, which is broken for you: this do in remembrance of me. After the same manner also he took the cup when he had supped, saying, this cup is the new testament in my blood: this do ye, as oft as ye drink it, in remembrance of me. For as often as ye eat this bread and drink this cup, ye do shew the Lord's death till he come. Wherefore whosoever shall eat this bread, and drink this cup of the Lord, unworthily, shall be guilty of the body and blood of the Lord. But let a man examine himself, and so let him eat of that bread, and drink of that cup. For he that eateth and drinketh unworthily, eateth and drinketh damnation to himself not discerning the Lord's body."

This Protestant translation shows the harshest of penalties for receiving the Eucharist without recognizing (discerning) the Body of the Lord. The Eucharist is not ordinary food and drink to nourish the body; it is supernatural food and drink to nourish the soul. Receiving it as other than the Body, Blood, Soul and Divinity of Our Lord Jesus desecrates the Sacrament. It is like saying, "I believe Jesus lied when He said, "This is My Body... This is My Blood." Jesus died on the cross, so we could all have this universal meal to share as members of God's one family. By denying it, one makes Jesus' sacrifice on the cross meaningless for them.

THE BIBLE

Q. Why don't you bring Bibles to church?

Q. How often is the Bible read in the Catholic Church?

A. Protestant churches have Bibles in the backs of their pews and encourage their members to bring their own Bibles. Most Catholic parish churches provide missalettes in the backs of their pews which contain the readings from Holy Scripture which are to be proclaimed on a particular day. In this way, every person has the same translation to hear and read. Depending upon the parish, this could be from the New American Bible (NAB), the Jerusalem Bible (JB), or the Revised Standard Version, Catholic Edition (RSV-CE). The New Revised Standard Version, Catholic Edition (NRSV-CE) is not approved for liturgical use because of its use of inclusive language. Every parishioner is encouraged to bring their personal Bible with them for use in prayer and meditation before and after Mass.

Most non-Catholics are not aware that the Catholic Church has liturgical services every day of the year. They are also not aware that the Catholic Church has a liturgical calendar which determines which readings from Holy Scripture are to be proclaimed each and every day of the year. The Sunday readings are divided into 3 yearly cycles. Each contain some readings from the Gospels. Old Testament readings and responsorial Psalms are selected because of their relation to the Gospel reading, and New Testament epistles are proclaimed. Readings from the Book of Acts replace the Old Testament readings during the period of Easter. This liturgical calendar and cycle of readings has been adopted, with minor modifications, by both the Lutheran and Episcopal churches.

Likewise, the readings for weekday Masses are divided into 2 yearly cycles. Any day of the year a person can walk into a Catholic parish church anywhere in the world and hear the same readings proclaimed. If someone were to attend Mass every day for three years, they would hear approximately 98% of the New Testament and more than 85% of the Old Testament proclaimed from the pulpit. In addition to this, much of the Catholic Mass uses quotations from Holy Scripture. If someone were to use a stopwatch to determine the amount of time spent proclaiming Holy Scripture during a typical Mass, they would find that from the Greeting, "The grace of the Lord Jesus Christ and the love of God and the fellowship of the Holy Spirit be with you all (2 Corinthians 13:13)", to the Dismissal, "Thanks be to God (2 Corinthians 9:15)", more than 25% of the Mass is spent proclaiming Holy Scripture, not talking about it, but proclaiming it. No other denomination comes even close to this amount of time.

<u>Recommended Reading:</u>

Stravinskas, Rev. Peter M. J., *The Mass: A Biblical Prayer*, Our Sunday Visitor, Huntington, IN 46750, 1987.

Currie, David B., *Born Again Catholic, Born Fundamentalist*, Ignatius Press, San Francisco, CA, 94122, pp. 99, 408.

Q. What is the oldest written record of the Bible?

A. Let us begin this answer by stating that there are no original manuscripts (called autographs) of any of the books of the Bible; all have been lost or destroyed. All we have are copies, old copies, but copies nonetheless. Up until the discovery of the Dead Sea Scrolls in 1947, the oldest Old Testament manuscript was dated from around the year 900 A.D.

The Dead Sea Scrolls have been dated from around the time of Christ, give or take 100 years and contain parts from every book of the Hebrew Bible, except Esther. These scrolls include parts of many of the deuterocanonical books (Sirach, 1 & 2 Maccabees, Judith, Wisdom, Tobit & Baruch) as well, all in Hebrew. The oldest New Testament manuscripts are in Greek and date from around 350 A.D. There are many reasons for the destruction of early manuscripts including the facts that:

1. They were written on papyrus or animal parchment which degrade quickly;
2. When pagans invaded a town, they burned the churches and church libraries;
3. And as manuscripts became worn, they were copied, and then the worn copy was reverently destroyed.

Q. Why do you call your priests "Father" when the Bible says call no one father?

A. On occasion one will encounter a separated brethren who will criticize Catholics because they call their priest "father" citing Matthew 23:9 KJV:

> "And call no man your father upon the earth: for one is your Father, who is in heaven."

If one takes this passage literally and out of the context in which it is used in the Bible, this might seem to be a fair criticism.

What does a person call their male parent? Daddy? Papa (which, incidentally, is Italian for Pope)? When one fills out a credit application, what do they put in the block which asks for their father's name – God? Obviously, there is a meaning of this scriptural passage other than the literal one; this meaning is called the contextual meaning. In Matthew 23:9, Jesus is taking the Pharisees to task for requiring the people to perform rigorous tasks while avoiding these tasks themselves. The Pharisees were quick to accept places of honor and marks of public respect but were not making the burden of the people any lighter. They were not "fathering" or "teaching"; they were not Creator, from whom all "fatherhood" comes (Ephesians 3:14-15). We cannot claim the title of "father" or "teacher" if we do not emulate God's example. This passage does not preclude addressing someone as "father" so long as it is understood that all fatherhood (both biological and spiritual) originates with God the Father. We are all members of God's family; a fact we acknowledge every time we recite the Our Father or the Creed.

Now let's look at how the term "father" is used elsewhere in Holy Scripture: Paul calls himself a "father" in 1 Thessalonians 2:11 KJV:

> "As ye know how we exhorted and comforted and charged every one of you, as a father does his children."

And again, in 1 Corinthians 4:15 KJV:

> "For though ye have ten thousand instructors in Christ, yet have ye not many fathers: for in Christ Jesus, I have begotten you through the gospel."

In both of these passages Paul considers himself a spiritual father just as the priest is today. This same interpretation is presented by John where he says twice in 1 John 2:13-14 KJV:

> "I write unto you, fathers, because ye have known him that is from the beginning."

Stephen, in his address to the Sanhedrin (Acts 7:1-53), calls people "father" 17 times; he became the first Christian martyr not because of this, but because he was bearing the testimony of Christ.

Finally, one may point to the New International Version of the Bible (a common very good modern Protestant translation). Refer them to Matthew 23:10., the verse immediately after the one quoted about father. It says neither are you to be called "teacher," for you have one Teacher, the Christ. Even Protestants have Sunday School teachers.

Recommended Reading:

Pacwa, Mitchell S.J., "Call No Man Father?", *This Rock*, The Magazine of Catholic Apologetics & Evangelization, January 1991, pp. 17-19.

Mbukanma, Rev. Jude O, *Is it in the Bible?,* Scripture Keys Ministries Australia, Broadford, Victoria, Australia, 1987, p. 11.

Q. Why tradition, scripture, and teaching authority rather than just scripture?
Q. Does the Bible support the use of oral tradition?

A. Occasionally one will encounter an individual who says, "If it isn't in the Bible, I don't believe it." This presumes that everything Jesus said and did is recorded in the Bible. However, we all know that Jesus didn't make His graces dependent upon the ability to read or own a Bible. Jesus didn't command that His Apostles go and write down everything He had said so that people can read it. Rather, Jesus said, Go and baptize! Go and teach! (Matthew 28:19-20) His truths were to be spread, as was obviously necessary before the invention of the printing press, mainly by the spoken word. It is true that some of the Apostles and their companions did commit to writing many things about the life and doctrines of Our Lord. The oral teachings of the Apostles are just as truly the Word of God as their written words which we find preserved in the New Testament. This fact is evidenced by the following scriptural passages:

Where Jesus says,

> "'He who heareth you, heareth me.'" (Luke 10:16 KJV).

And,

> "And many other signs truly did Jesus in the presence of his disciples which are not written in this book." (John 20:30 KJV);

> "And there are also many other things which Jesus did, the which, if they should be written every one, I suppose that even the world itself could not contain the books that should be written." (John 21:25 KJV);

> "Therefore, brethren, stand fast, and hold the traditions which ye have been taught, whether by word or our epistle." (2 Thessalonians 2:15 KJV);

> "I have much to write to you, but I do not want to use paper and ink. Instead, I hope to visit you and talk with you face to face, so that our joy may be complete." (2 John 1:12 NIV);

> "I had many things to write, but I will not with ink and pen write unto thee: But trust I shall shortly see thee, and we shall speak face to face." (3 John 13-14 KJV).

These last two passages can be especially appreciated if one remembers that family members communicate best by talking to each other rather than passing notes back and forth. By the New Covenant all are made members of God's family (as opposed to belonging to His book-of-the-month club). The bare essentials to receive God's favor are contained in the Bible but this doesn't mean that God, in His loving generosity, has not provided abundantly far more for those who will avail themselves of it. Nor does it mean that everyone can read it to themselves and understand the words contained in the Bible, as Acts 8:30-31 so clearly enumerates in the story about the Ethiopian eunuch. Remember that 2 Timothy 3:16 says that all scripture is useful; it doesn't say or even imply that it is the exclusive source.

The point is that:

1. The Bible, Word of God that it is, doesn't claim to be the sole source of information but instead documents certain happenings and the establishment of a teaching authority within the Church which Jesus established; and
2. Dependence upon the Bible as the sole authority in essence says that Jesus' word is not to be trusted when Jesus says that He will be with His Church (as it baptizes and teaches) until the end of time (Matthew 28:20).

The Bible is not a catechism or theological treatise where one can go for quick easy answers. It's too bad that it isn't, but wishing it was (or pretending that it is) doesn't make it so. Attempting to use the Bible in this manner is to misuse Holy Scripture. The truth is there, but we must know how to get at it, as in many cases, it is not presented in a straightforward manner readily understandable to the 21st Century Christian. This is because the sacred writers depended heavily upon 1st century (and earlier) Jewish traditions, customs, and beliefs which are not necessarily recorded in the Bible. It is important that we also consult the other historical writings to find, and therefore learn, how the writings (now part of Holy Scripture but only important writings at that time) were understood and taught by those to whom the writings were addressed.

"If it isn't in the Bible, I don't believe it", may seem reasonable to the one saying it, but it is a self-contradicting statement because nowhere in the Bible does it say that the Bible is the exclusive authority. Thus, the person saying this believes something which is not in the Bible. In fact, the Bible says that the Church is the authority:

> "the church of the living God, the pillar and foundation of truth." (1 Timothy 3:15 NIV).

<u>Recommended Reading:</u>

Catechism of the Catholic Church, Libreria Editrice Vaticana, 1994, paras. 74-87.

Shea, Mark P., *By What Authority?*, Our Sunday Visitor, Huntington, IN 46750, 1996.

Currie, David B., *Born Fundamentalist, Born Again Catholic*, Ignatius Press, San Francisco, CA, 1996, pp. 51-62.

Hardon, John A., S.J., *The Catholic Catechism*, Doubleday, New York, NY,12020, 1981, pp. 41-52.

"Tradition, Bible, or both?", A Catholic Answers Tract, Catholic Answers, P. O. Box 17490, San Diego, CA 92177.

"What's Your Authority for That?", A Catholic Answers Tract, Catholic Answers, P.O. Box 17490, San Diego, CA 92177.

McGuinness, Msgr. Richard M. & Quill, Rev. John A., *Who Needs the Church? I Have a Bible,* A Defending the Faith Tract, World Apostolate of Fatima, Washington, NJ 07882, 1992.

Nunez, Luis S., *St. Paul's Scriptural Arguments for Tradition,* The Catholic Answer, Volume 10/Number 3, July/August 1996, pp. 32-35.

"Not by Scripture Alone", *This Rock,* The Magazine of Catholic Apologetics & Evangelization, November 1996, pp. 36-38.

Q. Please explain why, when on the cross and nearing death, Jesus said, "My God, My God, why have you forsaken me?" (Matthew 27:46)

A. Jesus, being God, could not have forsaken himself, nor is it possible for His human and divine natures to be separated with one talking to the other, so this is not a lament. The Jews of Jesus' time, not having bound copies of the Old Testament to carry around with them, studied the Word of God and committed it to memory.

The devout Jew would pray the Psalms and other Scriptures from memory as he worked and traveled. The sacred writers of the New Testament knew that if they included a key phrase from a Psalm or other sacred writing, the entire context would be brought to the mind of the listener (reader). If I were to say, "I pledge allegiance to the flag," any American hearer would immediately recall the rest of the pledge. "My God, My God, Why have you forsaken me?" are the opening words of Psalm 22 and Jesus, in praying this particular Psalm, was calling to the minds of all who heard Him the context of this Psalm; which foretold, in graphic detail, all that was happening to Him. It was a final reminder that He was the promised Messiah.

Recommended Reading:
Psalm 22

Q. A Protestant man once asked me why we did not read the Protestant Bible.
Q. Is the Catholic Bible the only real Bible?

A. The primary reason that Catholics don't read the Protestant Bible is that the Protestant Bible is incomplete. It has left out seven books of the Old Testament, along with parts of two others. The missing books are Judith, Tobit, 1 & 2 Maccabees, Wisdom, Sirach, and Baruch. Parts of Daniel and Esther have also been omitted. The reasons for the differences in the number of books in the Old Testament go back to around the year 90 A.D., even though there were no Protestants until 1517. It is said that, although there is no proof of it, that around the year 90 A.D. (some 60 years after Jesus' death and resurrection and 20 years after the destruction of The Temple in Jerusalem), a group of Pharisees decided that the Hebrew canon of Scripture would not contain the above-mentioned works because they did not meet certain criteria.

These criteria seem to have been:

1. Must have originally been written in Hebrew,
2. Must have their original composition dated prior to about 400 B.C.,
3. Must be of good moral character.

The Scriptures in common use in Palestine from about 200 years before the time of Jesus up until that time were a Greek version (called *Septuagint*) containing all the books, including those which did not meet these criteria. The *Septuagint* was used by the Apostles and continued to be used by the Catholic Christian Church after the supposed declaration of the Hebrew canon. At the time of the Protestant Reformation, the reformers decided to use the Hebrew canon for a variety of reasons, and the other books were omitted. The Revised Standard Version, Catholic Edition (commonly called the Ignatius Bible), is an excellent Protestant translation which has the omitted books restored and is approved for Catholic use.

<u>Recommended Reading:</u>

Graham, Right Rev. Henry G., *Where We Got the Bible,* TAN Books & Publishers, Rockford, IL 61105, 1977.

Keating, Karl, *Catholicism and Fundamentalism*, Ignatius Press, San Francisco, CA, 1988, pp. 121-133.

Q. Did Jesus drink wine, or was it grape juice?

A. Jesus drank wine. That said, let's look at the historical circumstances. Grapes are harvested in the fall, and Passover (the time of the Last Supper) is in the spring. Without refrigeration, grapes (and grape juice) do not keep very well. Within a few days after the harvest, grapes begin to ferment and/or rot. The only method of preservation available to the 1st century citizen was to extract the juice and let it ferment under somewhat controlled conditions (this is called wine making) or to dry the grapes which resulted in raisins. At the Last Supper Jesus said,

> "I will not drink henceforth of this fruit of the vine." (Matthew 26:29 KJV).

In those days they made wine from a number of different fruits but the wine of the grape, the "fruit of the vine," was alone used at Passover. Since this was spring, and the Passover liturgy called for all participants to drink four cups of wine, grape juice preserved by fermentation (wine), was most certainly used or at least one of the Gospel writers would have remarked about the departure from the natural; as they did so often about all His other miracles.

The prescriptions for celebrating the Passover called for the cups of wine to be diluted with water. This was necessary because the fermentation process made it rather strong, and also because the vessels they kept the wine in were somewhat porous. The wine tended to become thick with age as moisture escaped. This is the historical background behind why the priest adds a drop of water to the chalice during the Liturgy of the Eucharist. Wine, not well protected from the air while it was stored, became sour wine (vinegar).

Q. Why do we repeat prayers when in the Bible it says not to be repetitive?

Q. Isn't it a sin to repeat the same memorized prayers such as the Hail Mary and the Rosary?

A. The verse being referred to here is Matthew 6:7 KJV:

> "But when ye pray, use not vain repetitions, as the heathens do: for they think they shall be heard for their much speaking."

To best understand what is being said here, we must first determine what is meant by "vain." The dictionary says that vain means fruitless, worthless, conceited, or irreverent. The Hail Mary and the Rosary are none of these; we are praying for God's mercy now (since we acknowledge that we are sinners) and at the time of our death (when we will be most in need of God's mercy). How did the heathens pray? Their gods had many different names and the pagans weren't certain to which name their gods were responding on any given day, so they recited a litany of all the names to be sure that they got their god's attention – this is vain repetition. God hears us every time we pray.

To fully understand the context of Matthew 6:7, we must look at Matthew 6:5 NIV:

> "And when you pray, do not be like the hypocrites, for they love to pray standing in the synagogues and on the street corners to be seen by men."

Jesus was talking about those who pray in a manner designed to draw attention to themselves, not about sincere people who engage in repetitive prayer.

In the parable of the persistent widow (Luke 18:1-8), Jesus told His disciples that they should always pray and not give up. We all repeat our prayers, sometimes a few seconds apart and sometimes weeks apart. There is nothing in Holy Scripture that says we should change our words or thoughts each time we pray. In the parable, the persistent widow was praised by Jesus for her dogged repetition of her prayer requests. God in heaven is continually praised with the repetition of words, as we see by the following:

> "Day and night they never stop saying: 'Holy, holy, holy is the Lord God Almighty, who was, and is, and is to come.'" (Revelation 4:8 NIV).

Finally, Jesus Himself repeated the same prayer three times during His Agony in the Garden (Matthew 26:39, 42, 44) when He asked that the cup pass from Him. There is a big difference between vain repetition and sincere repetition of prayer.

<u>Recommended Reading:</u>

Rumble, Rev. Dr. Leslie & Carty, Rev. Charles Mortimer, *Radio Replies, First Volume*, TAN Books & Publishers, Rockford, IL 61105, 1979, paras. 1423-1425.

Q. What about nuns? They are nowhere in the Bible.

A. Neither are airplanes, telephones, or Protestants. Airplanes, telephones and Protestants are recent developments, but the concept of consecrated virginity is shown in: 1 Corinthians 7:34 NIV:

> "An unmarried woman or virgin is concerned about the Lord's affairs; Her aim is to be devoted to the Lord in both body and spirit. But a married woman is concerned about the affairs of this world – how she can please her husband."

Actually, the consecrated life has been part of the true religion since before the time of Christ. In the Old Testament there was an entire order of men and women, known as "Nazarites" (consecrated ones), who were essentially monks and nuns. They took vows of self-denial and had a distinctive appearance.

St. Paul set up an order of widows living the consecrated life after the deaths of their husbands:

> "Give proper recognition to those widows who are really in need. But if a widow has children or grandchildren, these should learn first of all to put their religion into practice by caring for their own family and so repaying their parents and grandparents, for this is pleasing to God. The widow who is really in need and left all alone puts her hope in God and continues night and day to pray and to ask God for help. But the widow who lives for pleasure is dead even while she lives. Give the people these instructions, so that no one may be open to blame. Anyone who does not provide for his relatives, and especially for their own household, has denied the faith and is worse than an unbeliever. No widow may be put on the list of widows unless she is over sixty, has been faithful to her husband and is well known for her good deeds, such as bringing up children, showing hospitality, washing the feet of the Lord's people, helping those in trouble and devoting herself to all kinds of good deeds. As for younger widows, do not put them on such a list. For when their sensual desires overcome their dedication to Christ, they

> want to marry. Thus, they bring judgement on themselves, because they have broken their first pledge." (1 Timothy 5:3-12 NIV).

<u>Recommended Reading:</u>

Catechism of the Catholic Church, Libreria Editrice Vaticana, 1994, paras. 1618-1620.

"Monks and Nuns", *This Rock*, The Magazine of Catholic Apologetics & Evangelization, March 1996, pp. 43-45.

Rumble, Rev. Dr. Leslie & Carty, Rev. Charles Mortimer, *Radio Replies, First Volume,* TAN Books & Publishers, Rockford, IL 61105, 1979, paras. 1216-1258.

Q. Evolution or creation: Which is right and why?

Q. Where did Cain and Abel go to meet other people, and where did these other people come from?

Q. How literally should the Bible be interpreted?

A. God is the divine author of Sacred Scripture. Under the inspiration of the Holy Spirit human authors composed the sacred books; making full use of their own faculties and powers to convey whatever God wanted written, and no more. The books of the Bible firmly, faithfully, and without error teach that truth which God, for the sake of our salvation, wished to see written down.

The Bible can be very difficult to understand if we read it like a novel. It is not a continuous narrative, a science book, nor is it a comprehensive history of the world. The Bible does not tell us how God did what He did, but it does tell us why He did it. The creation accounts in Genesis are a good example. There is not enough information contained in these first two chapters to determine how God made the world and populated it, or even when He started and how long it took. Did God create everything just as it looks today or did changes take place after they were first created? We don't know because that was not the reason these chapters were written. These chapters were written to show that God was the origin of everything and that without God, nothing could or would exist. In 1950, Pope Pius XII allowed that evolution was a serious theory and could be studied and promoted without Catholic opposition, provided it was not presented as a certainty and that it was given in terms compatible with the faith.

In 1996, Pope John Paul II stated that evolution should be recognized as "more than a hypothesis." This doesn't mean that evolution is a fact, just that it is a theory which has some scientific evidence to support it and as such it is to be studied seriously. As Catholics, we are free to believe either that God created it as we see it, or that things evolved; neither belief is a matter of faith. However, we are required to believe that God was the origin of it all because of His infinite love, that we have all descended from the one pair of first parents, and that the soul is just as God breathed it into mankind; the soul did not evolve.

The story of Cain and Abel is not about how the human race was propagated; it is about the effect of Original Sin and the fact that this effect was carried on to subsequent generations.

To interpret the Bible correctly we must be aware of what the human authors wanted to affirm and what God wanted to tell us in their words. To do this we must be aware, among other things, of the conditions of the author's time and culture as well as the literary styles and methods of speaking which were then current. Because it is inspired writing, we must read and interpret the Bible in the light of the same Holy Spirit who inspired it. Finally, because Jesus entrusted His people to His Church and not to a library of books, we must interpret the Bible within the living Tradition of that Church; if an interpretation is not in accordance with the teaching of the Catholic Church, the interpretation is in error and must be discarded.

All this may sound discouraging, but rest assured that reading the Bible can be refreshing and enjoyable. Many insights can be gained into what God wants from us and how He works in us.

There are many good books available to help us understand the Bible better, and there are Catholic Bible studies available. All it takes is a commitment of time.

Recommended Reading:

Catechism of the Catholic Church, Libreria Editrice Vaticana, 1994, paras. 101-119, 337-349.

Kreeft, Peter, *You Can Understand the Old Testament: A Book-by-Book Guide for Catholics*, Servant Publications, Ann Arbor, MI, 48107, 1990.

Kreeft, Peter, *Reading and Praying the New Testament: A Book-by-Book Guide for Catholics*, Servant Publications, Ann Arbor, MI, 48107, 1992.

Most, Fr. William G., *Free from All Error,* Prow Books/Franciscan Marytown Press, Libertyville, IL, 60048, 1985.

Laux, Fr. John, *Introduction to The Bible,* TAN Books & Publishers, Rockford, IL 61105, 1990.

Fuentes, Antonio, *A Guide to The Bible,* Four Courts Press, Dublin/ Lumen Christi Press, Houston, TX, 1987.

Q. Please explain the doctrine of predestination.

A. The doctrine of predestination is: "God, by His eternal resolve of Will, has predestined certain men to eternal blessedness." This doctrine is based on Romans 8:29-30 NIV:

> "For those God foreknew he also predestined to be conformed to the image of his Son, that he might be the firstborn among many brothers and sisters. And those he predestined, he also called; those he called, he also justified; those he justified, he also glorified."

This doesn't mean that those so favored cannot cast aside their salvation if they so will, and those not so favored cannot still be saved. God desires the salvation of all mankind. This is shown in the beginning of Genesis where the man and the woman are in the garden, able to speak to God face-to-face. This is the destiny which God wants for us all. Like our first parents, we also have a free will to choose to obey Him or not. God doesn't interfere with that choice. This is why St. Paul tells us in Philippians 2:12 KJV:

> "...work out your own salvation with fear and trembling."

God has given each of us a free will, and He will do nothing to interfere with it. The Catholic teaching on predestination is in direct contrast to the teaching of Protestant reformer John Calvin which is described in his *Institutes of the Christian Religion* (1536):

> "God's eternal decree, by which he compacted with himself what he wills to become of each man. Eternal life is foreordained for some, eternal damnation for others. Therefore, as any man has been created to one or the other of these ends, we speak of him as predestined to life or to death."

In a nutshell, the Catholic teaching is that we all have a free will, and it is our use of this will that determines our salvation or damnation. Since God knows everything, He knows how we will turn out since He can read the last page in our book of life. God does not predestine certain individuals; the individuals, by their choices in life, make the determination.

Recommended Reading:

Meagher, Paul K. OP, O'Brien, Thomas C. & Aherne, Sister Consuelo M. SSJ, *Encyclopedic Dictionary of Religion*, Corpus Publications, Washington, D.C., 1979, pp. 2862-2865.

Q. Does God lead us into temptation (Matthew 6:13)?

A. The Lord's Prayer has been recited with this phrasing by Catholics since the 16th century. The translation we still use today was made by King Henry VIII of England (d. 1547) and imposed on all the churches in England by him. Even after Henry died and the troubles of the Reformation eased, Catholics have continued using his translation.

St. Matthew, no doubt, agrees with James:

> "When tempted, no one should say, 'God is tempting me.' For God cannot be tempted by evil, nor does he tempt anyone." (James 1:13 NIV).

And St. Mathews agrees with St. Paul that God can give an escape from temptation:

> "And God is faithful; he will not let you be tempted beyond what you can bear. But when you are tempted, he will also provide a way out so that you can endure it." (1 Corinthians 10:13 NIV).

God does not "lead" us into temptation. King Henry VIII did an accurate literal translation of the Greek and Latin forms, but it is difficult to translate from one language to another and retain the entire sense of what is being said. The Greek verb which was translated as "lead" can also be translated so that the passage reads "do not allow us to enter into temptation" or "do not let us yield to temptation." We have a free will and are faced with choices. We are asking for guidance in making the correct decisions.

Recommended Reading:

Catechism of the Catholic Church, Libreria Editrice Vaticana, 1994, paras. 2846-2849, 2863.

Q. Is Mary the woman in the Book of Revelation?

A. This probably refers to Revelation 12:1-5. Let's look at the passage in question:

> "And there appeared a great wonder in heaven; a woman clothed with the sun, and the moon under her feet, and upon her head a crown of twelve stars: And she being with child cried, travailing in birth, and pained to be delivered. And there appeared another wonder in heaven; and behold a great red dragon, having seven heads and ten horns, and seven crowns upon his heads. And his tail drew the third part of the stars of heaven and did cast them to the earth: and the dragon stood before the woman which was ready to be delivered, for to devour her child as soon as it was born. And she brought forth a man child, who was to rule all nations with a rod of iron: and her child was caught up unto God, and to his throne." (Revelation 12:1-5 KJV).

Since the earliest times of the Church, commentators have identified the woman with the ancient people of Israel, or the Church which Jesus Christ established, or with the Blessed Virgin Mary. The text supports all three interpretations, and none is a perfect fit. The woman can represent the people of Israel because it is from that people that the Messiah comes. Isaiah compares Israel to:

> "a woman with child, that draweth near the time of her delivery is in pain, and crieth out in her pangs." (Isaiah 26:17 KJV).

Using this same verse, the woman can represent the Church which Jesus Christ established because it is this people who are the people of God, the true Israel of the Old and New Testaments; primitive Christian writings made no clear distinction between Israel and the Church. Finally, the woman can represent the Blessed Virgin Mary because it is she who truly and historically gave birth to Jesus.

If I had to pick only one of the three interpretations, I would pick Mary for the following reasons: All commentators agree that Satan is represented by the dragon and the child which is born is Jesus the Messiah. If each of these two figures represent a single entity, why would the third figure, the woman, represent a people rather than a single being as well? The woman's crown represents the people of God; the 12 tribes of Israel, the 12 patriarchs, and the 12 Apostles.

She is crowned because she is the queen of heaven. The fact that the woman has a head and feet while in heaven points to a bodily assumption. The woman is clothed in the sun because it is the splendor of God's glory and the moon is at her feet because the brightness of the moon is changeable and is overshadowed by the glory.

<u>Recommended Reading:</u>

The Navarre Bible, Revelation, Four Courts Press, Dublin, Ireland, 1992, pp. 96-99.

Brown, R. E., Fitzmyer, J. A., & Murphy, R. E., *The Jerome Biblical Commentary, Volume II*, Prentice-Hall Inc., Englewood Cliffs, NJ, 1968, pp. 482-483.

GOD

Q. Why is God invisible? (Asked by an 8-year-old)

A. God is invisible because God is a living spirit and as such has no size or shape. If He had size or shape, He would have limits beyond which He would not exist. God has no limits because He is everywhere and in everything. Although He is invisible in the sense of size and shape, we can see Him in everything that is around us; He is the beauty in every flower and the firmness in every rock. Most importantly, we can see Him in everyone we meet because He is the goodness and love within them.

Q. I am not questioned about my faith, but about the existence of God.

A. Just about everyone, at some time or another, has had doubt about God's existence and how to demonstrate that existence. Most books on apologetics (explaining and defending the faith, not apologizing for believing) address this question in detail. Here, I will give a synopsis of a couple of the demonstrations.

The Design Argument. As we look around us, we see the order and beauty of nature that surrounds us. Could this order and beauty be the result of some intelligent design and conscious purpose, or just a random happening? If it were a random happening, why do all daisies look the same, why do all people have two eyes, why do things always fall down when we drop them rather than sometimes falling up or sideways? This intelligent design and conscious purpose is what we call God.

The Kalam Argument: Kalam is an Arabic word meaning "speech," but it has come to mean a certain type of philosophical reasoning. The argument, which has appeal to both Christians and Muslims, is this:

1. Whatever begins to exist has a cause for its coming into being.
2. The universe began to exist.
3. Therefore, the universe has a cause for its coming into being. We call this cause God.

Q. What is heaven like?

A. It is difficult to give a description of heaven because no one has seen it and come back to tell us what it is like. Even the Bible describes heaven by telling us what it isn't:

> "What no eye has seen, what no ear has heard, and what no mind has conceived – the things God has prepared for those who love him." (1 Corinthians 2:9 NIV).

Rather than looking at ways of demonstrating the existence of heaven, let's look at some of the alternatives:

1. **Atheist**: Since there is no God, there is no image of God (soul). When we die, our existence is over.

2. **Ancient Pagan**: After we die, we become ghosts inhabiting a gloomy, dark underworld.
3. **Pantheist:** We are all drops of the cosmic ocean. When we die the drop returns to the ocean; there is no individuality.
4. **Reincarnationist**: When we die, our soul gets another earthly, mortal body.
5. **Skeptic**: No one knows what happens after death.

As you can see, none of these come close to the Christian concept of heaven as a place of eternal joy in the presence of God.

<u>Recommended Reading</u>:

Catechism of the Catholic Church, Libreria Editrice Vaticana, 1994, paras. 33, 231, 326, 1023-1029.

Kreeft, Peter & Tacelli, Ronald K., *Handbook of Christian Apologetics,* InterVarsity Press, Downers Grove, IL 60515, 1994, pp. 45-88, 257-279.

Laux, Fr. John, M.A., *Catholic Apologetics,* TAN Books & Publishers, Rockford, IL 61105, 1990, pp. 1-24.

Kreeft, Peter, *Fundamentals of the Faith,* Ignatius Press, San Francisco, CA, 94122, 1988, pp. 24-53.

Q. I don't exactly know about the Blessed Trinity.
Q. Are the Father, Son, and Holy Spirit all one person?
Q. Are God and Jesus two different people?

A. The Blessed Trinity, like the other dogmas of the Catholic Church, is a belief that has been held since the teaching of Christ to the Apostles. The Trinity is not found clearly defined in any passage in Sacred Scripture, nor does the name "trinity" appear within its pages. However, in order to be considered "Christian", one must believe in the Trinitarian God. In the first centuries, the Church sought to clarify what the Trinity was by deepening its own understanding and by defending it against errors. In order to do this, the Church had to develop its own terminology which is reflected in the dogmatic statement: *In God there are 3 Persons, the Father, the Son, and the Holy Spirit. Each of the 3 persons possesses one Divine Substance.*

The term "substance" designates the divine being in its unity (there is only one God); it doesn't mean that God has a size or shape. The term "person" designates the Father, Son, and Holy Spirit (these persons are really distinct from each other).

Attempts to describe this relationship clearly always fall short. St. Patrick is credited with using the shamrock; one stem composed of three leaves. Others have used water; a material which exists as ice, liquid, and steam. No matter how it is described, the Trinity is three persons in one God.

Recommended Reading:

Catechism of the Catholic Church, Libreria Editrice Vaticana, 1994, paras. 232-256.

Sheed, F. J., *Theology for Beginners*, Servant Books, Ann Arbor, MI 48107, 1981, pp. 25-48.

Duggan, G. H., S.M., *Beyond Reasonable Doubt,* St. Paul Books & Media, Boston, MA 02130, 1987, pp. 55-86.

Q. How does God know where I am, and why does He love me? (Asked by a 6-year-old)

A. God knows where you are because God is everywhere. As King David said:

> "Where can I go from your Spirit? Where can I flee from your presence? If I go up to the heavens, you are there; if I make my bed in the depths [sheol], you are there." (Psalm 139:7-8 NIV)

God loves you because God is love (1 John 4:8, 16). Just as your parents love you because God gave you to them, God loves you because He gave you the very breath of life, your soul, and you are special to Him.

Q. Why would the Lord God on Jesus' death send Him to hell rather than a place other than hell?

A. This passage from the Apostles' Creed has always caused problems for English readers because of the use of the word "hell". 1 Peter 3:19-20 NIV says:

> "After being made alive, he went and made proclamation to the imprisoned spirits - to these who were disobedient long ago when God waited patiently in the days of Noah while the ark was being built. In it only a few people, eight in all, were saved through water, ..."

This abode of the dead is called "sheol" in Hebrew, hades in Greek, and "purgation" in Latin. Flavius Josephus, a Pharisee and Jewish historian writing sometime between 60 A.D. and 100 A.D., describes this place as the abode of those awaiting the opening of heaven, believed by the Pharisees to be closed until a time determined by God. This place is separated into two parts separated by a huge chasm; one part for the unjust and the other part (called the Bosom of Abraham) for the just. Holy Scripture calls this abode of the dead "hell" because the occupants were deprived of the vision of God. Jesus went there to bring the Gospel message of salvation to complete fulfillment. Christ's work of redemption applies to all men of all times (past and future) and all places. No one comes to the Father except through Christ (John 14:6). (See Apostles' Creed in Appendix.)

Recommended Reading:

Luke 16:19-31.

Catechism of the Catholic Church, Libreria Editrice Vaticana, 1994, paras. 631-637.

Whiston, William (translator), "An Extract Out of Josephus' Discourse to The Greeks Concerning Hades", *The Works of Josephus*, Hendrickson Publishers, Peabody, MA 01961, 1992, pp. 813-814.

Q. Man was made in the image of God. Was man made in the substance of God?

A. Man was made in the image and likeness of God in that God has created in each one of us a spiritual being, our soul. God's "substance" is His essential nature, His oneness. We are not God and do not share in His "substance."

Recommended Reading:

Catechism of the Catholic Church, Libreria Editrice Vaticana, 1994, paras. 355-368.

BIRTH CONTROL

Q. Why can't we practice birth control?
Q. Why can't Catholics use artificial birth control?
Q. Why is birth control wrong?
Q. When the natural method (Natural Family Planning) fails and you have a huge family why is birth control wrong or is it?

A. Birth control is a term which really means just the opposite of what it sounds like: if successful it results in no birth and no self-control. Artificial contraception was condemned as a sinful act by every major Christian denomination in the world, Protestant and Catholic, until 1930. This condemnation was based on the fact that other than abstinence early man had no method of preventing pregnancy except withdrawal (coitus interruptus). This practice, which is also called onanism, is condemned in Genesis (keep in mind that during this period in the history of mankind if a man died without having fathered a son, it was the duty of his brother to provide his brother's widow with an heir):

> "Er, Judith's firstborn, was wicked in the Lord's sight; so, the Lord put him to death. Then Judith said to Onan, 'Lie with your brother's wife and fulfill your duty to her as a brother-in-law to produce offspring for your brother.' But Onan knew that the offspring would not be his; so,

> whenever he lay with his brother's wife, he spilled his semen on the ground to keep from producing offspring for his brother. What he did was wicked in the Lord's sight; so, the Lord put him to death also." (Genesis 38:7-10 NIV).

In the 1930 Lambreth Conference, the Anglican Church declared that artificial contraception was not considered sinful "where there was a clearly identified moral obligation to limit or avoid parenthood." In other words, it was left totally up to the consciences of the individuals involved. Within a relatively few years, every Protestant denomination had stopped condemning artificial contraception. Today, most promote it.

Genesis 1:27-28a NIV says:

> "So, God created mankind in his own image, in the image of God he created them; male and female he created them. God blessed them and said to them. 'Be fruitful and increase in number; fill the earth and subdue it.'"

In the sex act in marriage, the couple is complying with God's command and is performing an act of re-creation; with God's help they are creating a new life. Sexual activity using artificial contraception is a deliberate act to derive sexual pleasure (mutual masturbation) while avoiding the natural result of such activity (see the chapter titled "SIN"). It is an act of recreation rather than re-creation as it is ordered toward self, rather than toward God. Within society at large since 1930, the divorce rate has steadily increased until it has reached approximately 50 percent of all marriages

Within marriages which consciously practice Natural Family Planning (NFP), the divorce rate is approximately 2 percent.

Recommended Reading:

Catechism of the Catholic Church, Libreria Editrice Vaticana, 1994, paras. 1652, 2368-2370.

Meagher, Paul K. OP, O'Brien, Thomas C. & Aherne, Sister Consuelo M. SSJ, *Encyclopedic Dictionary of Religion,* Corpus Publications, Washington, D.C., 1979, pp. 905-910.

Pope Paul VI, *Humane Vitae*, Encyclical Letter, 29 July 1968.

Q. Is there an alternate form of family planning, other than Natural Family Planning (NFP), that is approved by the Church for those who cannot, for medical reasons, practice NFP?

A. The only "approved" methods are NFP and abstinence; any form of artificial contraception is immoral because it frustrates the life-giving aspect of marital intercourse. Any medical condition which would necessitate the use of something other than NFP would dictate the practice of abstinence.

Q. Why does the Church oppose abortion?

Q. Does "the Pill" cause abortions?

A. The Fifth Commandment is "You shall not kill." Abortion is the act of killing an unborn child. From the very first moment of their existence, a human being must be recognized as having the rights of a person. One did not become a person the moment one was born, one became a person the instant he/she was conceived. This is most clearly pointed out in Luke 1:39-44 KJV:

> "And Mary arose in those days, and went into the hill country with haste, into a city of Juda: And entered into the house of Zacharias, and saluted Elisabeth. And it came to pass, that, when Elisabeth heard the salutation of Mary, the babe leaped in her womb, and Elisabeth was filled with the Holy Ghost: And she spake out with a loud voice, and said, 'Blessed art thou among women, and blessed is the fruit of thy womb. And whence is this to me, that the mother of my Lord should come to me? For, lo, as soon as the voice of thy salutation sounded in mine ears, the babe leaped in my womb for joy.'"

Mary has given her consent to become the mother of Our Lord and is less than seven days pregnant. She has gone to visit her cousin whom the angel has told her is six months pregnant. In this exchange of greetings between Mary and Elizabeth, we learn that an embryo has leaped for joy at the presence of zygote (to use the terms some medical people use to avoid saying "baby"). These aren't simply lumps of tissue, as the abortionist would have one believe, but unborn human beings who have an effect on those around them.

Abortion has been condemned since the earliest writings of the Church. The *Didache*, a first century writing, (also known as *The Teaching of the Lord to the Gentiles, Through the Twelve Apostles* or *The Teaching of the Twelve Apostles*) says:

> "You shall not murder. You shall not commit adultery. You shall not seduce boys. You shall not commit fornication. You shall not steal. You shall not practice magic. You

> shall not use potions. You shall not procure abortion, nor destroy a new-born child. You shall not covet your neighbor's goods. You shall not perjure yourself." (*Didache* 2:2-3).

Contraceptive drugs (including "the pill") act in three major ways:

1. The drugs prevent the release of the egg from the ovaries;
2. The drugs thicken the mucus in the reproductive tract, making it more difficult for the sperm to reach the egg;
3. And should the egg manage to be released and fertilized, thus forming a new human being (called zygote from the Greek word meaning joined), the drugs cause the wall of the uterus to prevent implantation, thus causing the new child to be aborted.

The moment the egg is fertilized, the resulting zygote is a different DNA from the mother. It is not a piece of flesh of the mother; it is a new human being. The new little human now has all the genetic information necessary to form. The zygote develops as it travels and normally reaches the uterus where it implants in about eight days. The zygote is called an embryo about the second to the eighth week after fertilization. After this time the embryo is called a fetus.

<u>Recommended Reading:</u>

Catechism of the Catholic Church, Libreria Editrice Vaticana, 1994, paras. 2270-2275.

Pope John Paul II, *Evangelium Vitae* (The Gospel of Life), Encyclical Letter, March 25, 1995.

Drummey, James, *Catholic Replies*, C R. Publications, Norwood, MA 02062, 1995, pp. 335-380.

Q. Why can't our Priest tell people in the parish more about abortions, and that it should result in excommunication if Catholics vote for officials that are pro-choice?

A. I agree that more should be said about abortion and the Church penalties involved. On the other hand, it is fortunate also that the Church requires the homilist to address the readings for that particular day. This precludes him from talking, week after week, about whatever his favorite subject might be. There are several Sunday readings each year which afford an opportunity to address the issue of abortion.

Persons procuring a completed abortion, and all those involved in the deliberate and successful effort to bring about the completed abortion, are automatically excommunicated; provided that each person knew the Church's penalty for this action and went ahead with it anyway. Pope John Paul II says:

> "The excommunication affects all those who commit this crime with knowledge of the penalty attached and thus includes those accomplices without whose help the crime would not have been committed. By this reiterated sanction, the Church makes clear that abortion is a most serious and dangerous crime, thereby encouraging those who commit it to seek without delay the path of

> conversion. In the Church, the purpose of the penalty of excommunication is to make an individual fully aware of the gravity of a certain sin and then to foster genuine conversion and repentance" (*Evangelium Vitae*, n. 62)

As to whether voting for a person who is pro-choice results in automatic excommunication, Bishop John Myers of Peoria, IL, in his 1 June 1990 pastoral letter, *The Obligations of Catholics and the Rights of Unborn Children*, writes:

> "A public official who would deny unborn children the protection of laws enjoyed by other citizens is guilty of grave injustice. Ordinarily it is morally illicit to help such a person achieve an office in which he or she will be in a position to do such an injustice. Those who assist such candidates because of their position on abortion are guilty of complicity in the abortions their election would make possible . . . One is formally complicit in the injustice of abortion when one votes for a candidate even partially on the basis of his or her pro-abortion positions . . . One who supports legal abortion cannot avoid formal complicity by maintaining that he or she wills not abortion as such, but only the freedom of others to choose abortion. Anyone who supports legal abortion seeks to remove from one class of human beings a basic protection afforded to others. By helping to make abortion available, a person becomes formally complicit in its basic injustice whether or not he or she would actively encourage anyone else to have

an abortion. From the ethical point of view, there is no distinction between being "pro-choice" and being "pro-abortion". … All formal cooperation in abortion is gravely immoral. So is most material cooperation in abortion."

In other words, any Catholic who votes for a candidate because of the candidate's position on abortion is guilty of an objectively grave immoral action. The subjective sinfulness of the action depends, as always, on whether the voter acted with sufficient reflection and with full consent of the will.

Recommended Reading:

Drummey, James J., *Catholic Replies,* C. R. Publications, Norwood, MA 02062, 1995, pp. 359-365.

THE PAPACY

Q. When Jesus told Peter, "Upon this rock I will build my church," is Jesus the rock or is Peter?

A. The passage being referred to is Matthew 16:18, and it is Jesus who promises to do the building on the rock which is Peter. To better understand what is being said, let's look at the verse in its larger context.

> "When Jesus came to the region of Caesarea Philippi, he asked his disciples, 'Who do people say the Son of Man is?' They replied, 'Some say John the Baptist; others say Elijah; and still others, Jeremiah or one of the prophets.' 'But what about you?' he asked. 'Who do you say I am?' Simon Peter answered, 'You are the Messiah, the Son of the living God.' Jesus replied, 'Blessed are you, Simon, son of Jonah, for this was not revealed to you by man, but by my Father in heaven. And I tell you that you are Peter [Peter means rock] and on this rock I will build my church, and the gates of Hades [hell] will not overcome it [not prove stronger than it]. I will give you the keys of the kingdom of heaven; whatever you bind on earth will be [have been] bound in heaven, and whatever you loose

> on earth will be [have been] loosed in heaven.'" (Matthew 16:13-19 NIV – brackets contain footnoted interpretations from NIV text).

"Christ" means "anointed one." At the time of Jesus, the term "anointed one" had become synonymous with "king". By declaring Jesus to be the "Son of the living God," Simon has directed attention away from kingship (who would lead the people to victory on earth and liberate them from the Romans) to his divine relationship with God. This is the revelation to which Jesus refers when he says, "this was not revealed to you by man. …" Peter had just shown that God the Father is using him as an instrument of His revelation.

Only in this place in the four gospels is Simon identified as "son of Jonah"; in the two other occurrences where his father is identified, he is identified as John (John 1:42 and 21:15-17). Jesus has just used the title "Son of Man" for himself, which means "one like a man"; could it be that Jesus is saying that Simon is to be "one like Jonah?" Jonah was the one who preached the impending destruction of Nineveh and effected the repentance of the people. This was an early type of the role which Peter was to play in the Church, leading people to reconciliation with God.

"Peter" means "rock" as the footnote indicates. The Aramaic (the language Jesus spoke) word is 'kepha' which is transliterated in some texts as "Cephas" (John 1:42; 1 Corinthians; Galatians). Some will argue that the Greek text of Matthew has "petros" (pebble) for "Peter" and "petras" (large rock) for "rock" but this is inconsequential. In the time of Jesus, the two words were used interchangeably, the distinction being that "petras" is the feminine form of the word and as such it is not applied to a male. Christianity has enough problems without inferring Peter was effeminate. Since Jesus spoke Aramaic and "kepha" is not gender specific, the word play is obvious, unlike the English where "Peter" is substituted for "rock." This name change is very significant because no one had ever been named "rock" before; it's like naming the anchor man on your tug-of-war team "post"; it signifies what he is to do.

In the four gospels, the Greek word "ekklesia", translated here as "church" appears only twice; as in Matthew 16:13-19 above and in Matthew 18:17 NIV:

> "If they refuse to listen, tell it to the church; and if they refuse to listen even to the church, treat them as you would a pagan or tax collector."

From this, it is clear that the term "ekklesia" applies to the visible gathering of the community of Christians.

From the above discussion, it is clear that it is Jesus who was promising to establish a visible Church on earth with Peter, the Rock, as its visible earthly anchor. The Church was not to be established on Peter's faith, which we know faltered when he denied Jesus 3 times, but upon Peter, the individual who was leader of the Apostles and an instrument of the Father's revelation. As it says in Ephesians 2:20 NIV:

> "Built on the foundation of the apostles and prophets, with Christ Jesus himself as the chief cornerstone."

Although this answers the question, let's look at the rest of the scripture passages from Matthew 16:

1. "The gates of Hades will not overcome it," means very simply, that death will not overtake the Church. Hades, translated in the footnote as "Hell" was the abode of the dead, Abraham's bosom. It was the place where the souls of the just went after their earthly life because heaven was not yet open (this event happened with Jesus' death on the cross). When Peter died, the role of leader would be taken by another; the office would not cease when the occupant died. This means that there will always be a visible head who, like Peter, will be an instrument of the Father's revelation and guidance; Satan will not be able to expropriate the office because it is divinely protected. This type of perpetual office is not foreign to the Holy Scriptures: Isaiah 22:19-21 describes the replacement of Shebna with Eliakim as the head of the palace of the house of David; and Acts 1:20 describes where Peter, as head of the Apostles, calls for a replacement for the position which had been occupied by Judas Iscariot ("his bishoprick let another take", KJV).
2. The "keys of the kingdom of heaven" are the symbol of authority given only to the most trusted servant. Again, this is not an image which is foreign to Holy Scripture: It is used in Isaiah 22:22 where Eliakim is given the key to the house of David (a perpetual office since David has been dead for several hundred years), and in Revelation 1:18 where Jesus, who will judge us, is depicted as holding the keys of death and Hades.

3. Finally, the "binding" and "loosing": Very simply put, he who has the ability to bind and loose, has the ability to make the rules. As the visible head of the Church on earth, Peter is given the ability to make the earthly rules for the operation of this Church. This doesn't mean that he can change the rules that we have received from God (such as the ten commandments and all the others contained in Holy Scripture), but he can make such determinations as the length of the fast before receiving communion and whether priests should be allowed to marry. This binding and loosing also has an Old Testament parallel in Isaiah 22:22 where Eliakim, having received the keys, has the power of the keys explained "what he opens, no one can shut, and what he shuts, no one can open."

This means that Eliakim alone among the servants has the ability to determine who is admitted and who is excluded from the house (kingdom) of David. The authority to "bind and loose" is also given to the Apostles in Matthew 18:18, with one significant difference: Only Peter has been given the "keys", the symbol of ultimate authority.

Recommended Reading:

Catechism of the Catholic Church, Libreria Editrice Vaticana, 1994, paras. 440, 442-443, 552-553, 765, 881, 1444.

Jaki, Stanley L., *And on This Rock,* Trinity Communications, Manassas, VA, 1987, pp. 71-92.

Q. Explain Pope as successor of Peter.
Q. What is the exact role of the Pope?
Q. Why do Catholics think they have to have a Pope as a leader?

A. Because this is the way Jesus set it up. As explained in the answer to the preceding question, the office of Peter, the visible head of the Church on earth, was created by Jesus and given the promise that the gates of Hades would not prevail against it. This means that the office will remain, even after the occupant has gone to his eternal reward. The Lord Jesus is the one who gave His Apostles the responsibility to bind and loose and is also the one who does the building. In this action He endowed His community with a structure that is to remain until the Kingdom is fully achieved. The Apostles recognized this because they elected the successor for Judas (Acts 1:15-26).

If there were no visible head (successor of Peter) and bishops (successors of the Apostles) to support him, anarchy and chaos would result. Without the visible and physical presence of the successors of Peter and the Apostles to continually interpret and apply what Jesus left us, we would not be of one faith (Ephesians 4:5). If there were no visible leadership, it would be like giving the people of the United States the Constitution and Bill of Rights and after President Washington dies saying, "you're on your own now: no president, no congress, and no supreme court; may the spirit of Jefferson be with you." As evidence of this, just look at the more than 34,000 Protestant denominations which currently exist without a commonality of faith.

Recommended Reading:

Catechism of the Catholic Church, Libreria Editrice Vaticana, 1994, paras. 765, 816, 861-862.

Ripley, Canon Francis J., "Peter and His Successors", *This Rock,* The Magazine of Catholic Apologetics & Evangelization, June 1993, pp. 27-29.

Currie, David B., *Born Fundamentalist, Born Again Catholic,* Ignatius Press, San Francisco, CA, 1996, pp. 63-97.

Q. Does the Pope have special power and why?

Q. Is the Pope able to make new rules for the Church? If so, why?

A. The special "power" (authority and responsibility would be a better term) which the Pope has is called the "power of the keys". If Jesus hadn't given Peter this authority and responsibility, Peter and his successors would not have been able to make any rules or make any application of the Holy Scriptures to our daily lives. As explained in the answer to the first question in this section, the authority to bind and loose was given first to Peter, along with the keys to the kingdom of heaven (his badge of office, so to speak), and then later to the Apostles as a group. When acting together, the bishops (successors of the Apostles) make rules which are binding on the universal (meaning catholic) Church; provided the Pope (successor of Peter) approves the rules using the authority and responsibility given him by the "power of the keys".

The Pope can also exercise the "power of the keys" in making what is called an infallible pronouncement which is binding on the universal (catholic) Church. There have been two such pronouncements in modem times: the dogma of the Immaculate Conception of the Blessed Virgin Mary by Pope Pius IX in 1854, and the dogma of the Assumption of the Blessed Virgin by Pope Pius XII in 1950.

Individual bishops also exercise their authority to bind and loose as they lead their respective dioceses on a daily basis.

Recommended Reading:

Catechism of the Catholic Church, Libreria Editrice Vaticana, 1994, paras. 888-890.

Q. Please explain Papal Infallibility.

Q. I don't understand the Infallibility of the Pope and Church dogma.

A. As stated in the answer to the previous question, the Pope can exercise the "power of the keys" in making what is called an infallible pronouncement which is binding on the universal (catholic) Church. Infallibility means that the Pope is preserved from error when, as supreme pastor and teacher of all the faithful, he proclaims by a definitive act a doctrine pertaining to faith and morals.

Infallibility does not mean that the Pope cannot sin. The Holy Father goes to the Sacrament of Confession frequently and acknowledges his sinfulness at Mass when he says, "I confess to almighty God and to you, my brothers and sisters ...", and again, when he washes his hands prior to the Eucharistic prayer while asking God to "wash away my iniquity, cleanse me from my sins." Likewise, infallibility does not mean that the Pope cannot make a mistake when he talks about mathematics, science, or some other nonreligious matter.

To teach infallibly, the Pope must be teaching on faith or morals; he must speak with his full authority as the Successor of Peter and head of the universal Church on earth; he must make a final pronouncement on a doctrine at issue, and he must bind all the faithful to accept his teaching or fall away entirely from the divine and Catholic faith. Personal correspondence, even that in which a sensitive issue is addressed, is not infallible because it is not meant to bind all the faithful.

That Jesus intended to preserve Peter and his successors from error can be found in Our Lord's statement to Peter:

> "'Whatever you bind on earth will be [have been] bound in heaven, and whatever you loose on earth will be [have been] loosed in heaven.'" (Matthew 16.19 NIV - brackets contain footnoted interpretations from NIV text).

Jesus would hardly give approval in heaven to bad decisions by Popes on earth, so He provided protection against this happening. And what was this protection? It can be found in Matthew 28:20 KJV, where Jesus promised that,

> "'I am with you always, even unto the end of the world.'"

And again, in John 14:16-17 NIV, where Our Lord says,

> "'I will ask the Father, and he will give you another Advocate to help you and be with you forever - the Spirit of truth.'"

This Spirit of truth, the Holy Spirit, has been with the Catholic Church since Pentecost. History shows that during the past almost 2,000 years, no pope has ever made a false pronouncement on faith or morals. No dogma has ever been changed. Some have been refined to provide better definition, but the core thrust, and effect of the dogmatic statement has never changed.

<u>Recommended Reading:</u>

Catechism of the Catholic Church, Libreria Editrice Vaticana, 1994, paras. 891-892.

Drummey, James J., *Catholic Replies,* C. R. Publications, Norwood, MA 02062, 1995, pp. 71-74.

Ripley, Cannon Francis J., "Infallibility", *This Rock,* The Magazine of Catholic Apologetics & Evangelization, March 1993, pp. 21-23.

Q. Please explain the hierarchy of the Church as it relates to the authority for following doctrine.

A. The doctrine of the Catholic Church comprises all those teachings in faith and morals entrusted to the Church by Christ through the Apostles and given to us for the sake of our salvation. As such, doctrine is interchangeable with the whole of revelation. Some doctrines (such as the Trinity) have resulted from definitions which have come from Councils and confirmed by papal authority while others have resulted from papal definitions (such as the Immaculate Conception). Most of these definitions have been formulated in response to heterodox challenges to a particular doctrine. Defined doctrines are not optional and are the authentic teachings of the Church.

The teaching office of the Church, called the magisterium, was established by Jesus the Christ when He promised:

> "'I will ask the Father, and he will give you another Advocate to help you and be with you forever – the Spirit of truth, whom the Father will send in my name, will teach you all things and will remind you of everything I have said to you.'" (John 14:16-17,26 NIV).

The Magisterium rests with the Pope and the Bishops in communion with him.

Recommended Reading:

Catechism of the Catholic Church, Libreria Editrice Vaticana, 1994, paras. 84, 90, 175, 234, 888-892.

Stravinskas, Rev. Peter M. J., *Our Sunday Visitor's Catholic Encyclopedia,* Our Sunday Visitor, Huntington, IN 46750, 1991, pp. 321, 615.

Meagher, Paul K. OP, O'Brien, Thomas C. & Aherne, Sister Consuelo M. SSJ, *Encyclopedic Dictionary of Religion,* Corpus Publications, Washington, D.C., 1979, p. 2209.

Q. Are Catholics required to follow the Pope's teaching on moral issues, or only his teaching on doctrine?

A. All doctrinal teachings involve the issues of faith and morals. Although every encyclical letter addressed to the world on matters of faith and morals is not an infallible pronouncement, if the Pope restates a long-held teaching of the Church (for example; the evil of artificial contraception or that priestly ordination is reserved to men) a good case can be made for the infallibility of that restatement, even if the Pope does not specifically identify his encyclical as infallible, since he is definitively proclaiming that a certain doctrine of faith or morals is to be believed.

Catholics cannot disregard non-infallible statements from the Pope or their Bishop. Divine assistance is given to the Pope and the bishops in communion with him when they, as part of their ordinary teaching duties, propose a teaching that leads to a better understanding of divine revelation in matters of faith and morals. The faithful are to submit humbly and adhere sincerely to the teachings of the Pope, even when he is not speaking infallibly, because his ordinary teaching is an extension of his special gift from God.

Recommended Reading:

Catechism of the Catholic Church, Libreria Editrice Vaticana, 1994, para. 892.

Q. Did a reliable prophet really predict that Pope John Paul II is our last Pope?

A. No. St. Malachy (1095-1148) was a holy and dedicated bishop who restored religious fervor to Ireland in the 12th century. He is reputed to have performed miracles, and he died in the arms of St. Bernard at Clairvaux. St. Malachy is best known today however, for his alleged prophecies about those who would be Pope from the time of Celestine II (died 1144) to the end of the world.

According to the alleged list of St. Malachy, which was not discovered until more than 400 years after his death, there would be

112 popes after Celestine (the 165th Pope) ending with the only one listed by name, Peter the Roman; the rest being described by short phrases such as "Apostolic Pilgrim" and "Pastor and Sailor". Since John Paul II was the 263rd successor of St. Peter, this would leave 11 Popes, yet to be elected after him, before Peter the Roman.

The smartest thing to do is to recall the words of Our Lord:

> "'But about that day or hour, no one knows. not even the angels in heaven, nor the Son, but only the Father.'" (Matthew 24:36 NIV).

> "'Therefore, keep watch, because you do not know on what day your Lord will come.'" (Matthew 24:42, NIV).

Recommended Reading:

Drummey, James J., *Catholic Replies,* C. R. Publications, Norwood, MA 02062, 1995, pp. 77-78.

Q. Someone at work told me they read in one of the news magazines that Pope John Paul was quoted as saying he would be the last Pope. The Pope that followed would be the antichrist.
Q. I have heard that it has been a message from Our Lady that he would be the last Pope.

A. None of this has any bearing in truth. At the end of every millennium a certain hysteria breaks out. People become convinced that the end of the world is imminent. When this happens, rumors, such as those in this question, abound. Similar hysteria accompanied the arrival of the year 1000. As was said in the preceding answer, the smartest thing to do is to recall the words of Our Lord:

> "'But about that day or hour, no one knows, not even the angels in heaven, nor the Son, but only the Father.'" (Matthew 24:36 NIV).

> "'Therefore, keep watch, because you do not know on what day your Lord will come.'" (Matthew 24:42 NIV).

To this might also be added St. Paul's admonition:

> "…work out you own salvation with fear and trembling." (Philippians 2:12 KJV).

We must all approach each day as if it may be our last.

Q. What is a conclave?

A. A conclave is a closed meeting of the cardinals for the purpose of electing a pope. The word literally means a room closed with a key. The practice of having the meeting take place behind locked doors was initiated by Pope Gregory X in 1274 for the purposes of eliminating any outside interference and also to hasten the process, since his own election took almost three years, during which time a vacancy existed in the papacy. On February 22, 1996, Pope John Paul II issued the Apostolic Constitution *Universi Dominici Gregis* (On the Vacancy of The Apostolic See and The Election of The Roman Pontiff) which establishes the rules for the election of his successor. The election takes place in the Sistine Chapel. The maximum number of Cardinal electors must not exceed 120 and no Cardinal who has reached the age of 80 on or before the day before the Pope's death is allowed to vote. Assuming one ballot on the first day of the conclave and two ballots on each succeeding voting day, for the first 33 ballots a two-thirds majority is required to elect a new pope and after 33 ballots an absolute majority is required. All ballots and notes are burned at the end of each voting day with black smoke indicating that no new pope has been elected and white smoke indicating that a successor has been elected.

Recommended Reading:

Pope John Paul II, *Universi Dominici Gregis* (Apostolic Constitution On the Vacancy of The Apostolic See and The Election of The Roman Pontiff), February 22, 1996.

Q. What proof is there that Peter was the first Pope?

A. The best "proof" is Holy Scripture. However, no "proof" is sufficient if the person doesn't want to believe. In Matthew 16:18, Our Lord promised to build His Church on Peter, the Rock (see the first question in this section). In John 21:15-17 NIV, Jesus, the Good Shepherd, turns His flock over to Peter with the admonition to "Feed my lambs … Take care of my sheep … Feed my sheep". In Acts 15:7, at the Council in Jerusalem, it is Peter who provides the solution and ends the discussion on the problem of how to admit Gentiles into the Church. Throughout the Bible whenever the Apostles are listed, Peter is always listed first; an indication of his primacy.

There are some who have claimed that Peter was never in Rome and therefore never was the Bishop of Rome. This claim has pretty much died out in the past 50 years as archaeological excavations directly under the high altar of St. Peter's Basilica have unearthed a tomb which matches the description of the one in which Peter was reported to have been buried, complete with inscriptions referring to Peter. In the summer of 1968 Pope Paul announced that the skeletal remains of Saint Peter had been found and satisfactorily identified.

Recommended Reading:

Walsh, John Evangelist, *The Bones of Saint Peter,* Fount Paperbacks, Bungay, Suffolk, Great Britain, 1984.

Q. Was there a female Pope?

A. No. Some time ago some misguided writers wrote of a "Pope Joan" who was supposed to have reigned from 855 to 857. *The Encyclopedia Britannica* says that she is pure myth. *The Oxford Dictionary of the Popes,* written by J. N. D. Kelly (a Protestant) says the legend of a woman pope "scarcely needs painstaking refutation today, for not only is there no contemporary evidence for a female Pope at any of the dates suggested for her reign, but the known facts of the respective periods make it impossible to fit one in".

Recommended Reading:

This Rock, The Magazine of Catholic Apologetics & Evangelization, December 1990, p. 25.

Rumble, Rev. Dr. Leslie & Carty, Rev. Charles Mortimer, *Radio Replies, First Volume,* TAN Books & Publishers, Rockford, IL 61105, 1979, para. 455.

Madrid, Patrick, *Pope Fiction,* Basilica Press, San Diego, CA, 1999, pp. 167-177.

Q. Was there ever a false pope?

A. Yes. There have been several periods of time in the history of the Church where more than one person claimed to be pope at the same time. Those individuals who were not legitimately elected are called anti-popes (false popes) and there have been about 39 of them. The first was about the year 252 after the persecution by Roman Emperor Decius. Once the persecution ended a dispute arose about whether those who had denied their faith could be readmitted to the Church. Pope Cornelius and Bishop Cyprian of Carthage taught that bishops could grant God's forgiveness even for serious sins, like apostasy, even though the penances were long and severe. A party of rigorists, headed by the Roman priest Novatian, advocated permanent exclusion of all apostates from the Church. Claiming that Pope Cornelius had betrayed his trust, Novatian had himself elected as Pope by his followers.

The most memorable period lasted from 1378 to 1417 and is known as the Great Western Schism. During this period of time, Western Christendom was torn between two, and at times three, rival claimants to the papacy. Each of the rival claimants reflected national interests with the division initially taking place shortly after the death of Pope Gregory XI and the election of Urban VI as his successor. The disputes were finally resolved at the Council of Constance (1414-1417).

Recommended Reading:

Laux, Father John, *Church History,* TAN Books and Publishers, Rockford, IL 61105, 1989, pp. 71-72, 407-409.

Schreck, Alan, *The Compact History of the Catholic Church,* Servant Books, Ann Arbor, MI 48107, 1987, pp. 20-22, 56-57.

Ripley, Canon Francis J., "Peter and His Successors", *This Rock,* The Magazine of Catholic Apologetics & Evangelization, June 1993, pp. 27-29.

Meagher, Paul K. OP, O'Brien, Thomas C. & Aherne, Sister Consuelo M. SSJ, *Encyclopedic Dictionary of Religion,* Corpus Publications, Washington, D.C., 1979, pp. 1550-1551.

PURGATORY

Q. What is purgatory?
Q. Why do you believe in Purgatory?
Q. What proof do you have of the existence of Purgatory?

A. By "proof" it is assumed that the questioner is asking, "Where in the Bible does it say ...?" No one can "prove" the existence of anything, including even the existence of God or of heaven, if the person requesting the "proof" has already hardened their heart to the answer. In order to believe, the gift of faith must be present in the individual.

The word "purgatory" doesn't appear anywhere in Holy Scripture, neither do the words "trinity," "catholic," "protestant," nor "incarnation" but this fact doesn't preclude their existence. Catholic doctrine, based on our Jewish origins, is that at the moment of our death our soul, if perfect, goes straight to heaven; if not quite perfect, it goes to purgatory; if totally imperfect, it goes straight to hell. The concept of purgatory is certainly shown in Holy Scripture, so let's take a look at a few of the words of Jesus:

> "And whosoever speaketh a word against the Son of man, it shall be forgiven him: but whosoever speaketh against the Holy Ghost, it shall not be forgiven him, neither in this world, neither in the world to come." (Matthew 12:32 KJV).

> "Verily I say unto thee, Thou shalt by no means come out thence, till thou hast paid the uttermost farthing." (Matthew 5:26 KJV).

Both of these passages imply that some sins, not forgiven in this world, will be forgiven in the world to come. Is this "world to come" only heaven (the place of eternal joy) or is it possible that there is a place of purification (purgation) as well; a place where the uttermost farthing is paid? Again, let's look at a place in Holy Scripture where heaven is described:

> "Nothing impure will ever enter it, nor will anyone who does what is shameful or deceitful, but only those whose names are written in the Lamb's book of life." (Revelation 21:27 NIV).

Even if we have the smallest unrepented sin upon our soul, we are impure, defiled and cannot go straight to heaven. That is because this unrepented sin is a reflection of our pride, a lack of total dedication to God. It may be the smallest of all sins, but it still constitutes a stain upon our soul. So how do we get rid of it once we have passed into the "world to come"?

> "No one can lay any foundation other than the one already laid, which is Jesus Christ. If any man builds on this foundation using gold, silver, costly stones, wood, hay or straw, their work will be shown for what it is, because the Day will bring it to light. It will be revealed with fire, and the fire will test the

> quality of each person's work. If what has been built survives, the builder will receive a reward. If it is burned up, the builder will suffer loss; but yet will be saved – even though only as one escaping through the flames." (1 Corinthians 3:11-15 NIV).

> "For our God is a consuming fire (Hebrews 12:29) and For the Lord thy God is a consuming fire." (Deuteronomy 4:24 KJV).

These verses tell us, at our judgement after death, a purification takes place, and God does the purification. That which is unsuitable for heaven is consumed so that only that which is pure remains. Since at the moment of our death we pass from "this world" into the "world to come", this purification must take place in a place other than heaven. We call this place "purgatory", the place of purification. How long does this purification take? No one knows since when we leave "this world" we enter into the world where time has no domain, the Eternal Now.

Recommended Reading:

Catechism of the Catholic Church, Libreria Editrice Vaticana, 1994, paras. 1030-1032.

Rumble, Rev. Dr. Leslie & Carty, Rev. Charles Mortimer, *Radio Replies, First Volume,* TAN Books & Publishers, Rockford, IL 61105, 1979, paras. 951-969.

Q. Why do you pray for the dead?

A. Because we do not know how long the period of purification takes for any individual soul. The Bible which was used by all Christians until the 16th century says:

> "He also took up a collection, man by man, to the amount of two thousand drachmas of silver, and sent it to Jerusalem to provide for a sin offering. In doing this he acted very well and honorably, taking account of the resurrection. For if he were not expecting that those who had fallen would rise again, it would have been superfluous and foolish to pray for the dead. But if he was looking to the splendid reward that is laid up for those who fall asleep in godliness, it was a holy and pious thought. Therefore, he made atonement for the dead, so that they might be delivered from their sin." (2 Maccabees 12:43-45 RSV-CE).

God would not have inspired the Jews to pray for the dead if such prayers were of no avail. A prayer, called the Kaddish, which is prayed daily in the Synagogue services, has been prayed from before the time of Jesus until the present day. Jesus, the perfect Jew, nowhere condemns this practice, although He does take other practices to task; such as searching the Scriptures for answers instead of looking to Him (John 5:39). We pray for our loved ones, and all those whose souls are in purgatory, so that they may sooner enter heaven and behold the full glory of God.

> "'You study the Scriptures diligently because you think that in them you have eternal life. These are the very Scriptures that testify about me.'" (John 5:39 NIV).

Recommended Reading:

Rumble, Rev. Dr. Leslie & Carty, Rev. Charles Mortimer, *Radio Replies, First Volume,* TAN Books & Publishers, Rockford, IL 61105, 1979, paras. 970-992.

Q. Explain indulgences.

Q. What does it mean when they say 500 days indulgence?

A. An indulgence is the remission of the temporal punishments for sins, whether we sin against one another or against God directly. Once the sin has been forgiven, some restitution is necessary. If, for instance, I broke your window, knocked on your door and apologized and you forgave me, I would still be expected to pay for the repair of the window. If you told me that I did not have to pay for the window, or at least only for a part of it, you would have granted me an indulgence.

An indulgence is not a permission to commit sin; it is not even a forgiveness of past sins. An indulgence is concerned only with the debt of temporal punishment which we owe to God after our sins have been forgiven in the sacrament of penance (or by an act of perfect contrition).

The granting of indulgences is a doctrine in the Catholic Church, a doctrine whose application was very badly abused in the sixteenth century. The doctrine can be definitively traced back to the third century at which point it appears to be well established and is based scripturally on the power of the keys and the ability to bind and loose (see chapter titled "THE PAPACY").

The Church has exercised this power by remitting temporal punishment from the very earliest days of Christian history. In those early times, when Christians had a much greater horror of sin than we have nowadays, repentant sinners had to perform great penances before they would be readmitted to fellowship with the Christian community. A sinner might have to do public penance for forty days, or three years, or seven years, or even for the rest of his life – depending on the seriousness of his sins and the amount of scandal given. Examples of such penances were the wearing of rough sackcloth with ashes sprinkled on the head, fasting, scourging one's body, retiring to a monastery, kneeling at the church door to beg prayers from those entering, or wandering as a beggar through the countryside. When we see that an indulgence of 500 days is granted, this refers to the amount of temporal punishment which would have been imposed in the early Church.

Indulgences can be gained only for oneself or for those in purgatory. Indulgences cannot be gained for living persons other than oneself or for sins which have yet to be committed.

Recommended Reading:

Catechism of the Catholic Church, Libreria Editrice Vaticana, 1994, paras. 1471-1479, 1498.

Trese, Leo J., *The Faith Explained*, Sinag-Tala Publishers, Manila, Philippines, 1991, Copyright 1965 by Fides/Claretian, Notre Dame, IN, pp. 389-396.

Akin, James, "A Primer On Indulgences", *This Rock,* The Magazine of Catholic Apologetics & Evangelization, November 1994, pp. 13-21.

HEAVEN

Q. Should Catholics believe in the "rapture"?

Q. Do Catholics believe in the rapture that is referred to in Revelation?

A. In a single word, No. The "rapture" is an interpretation of Holy Scripture which is only about 130 years old. It is the idea that some believers will be snatched (raptured) up to Heaven at the second coming of Christ. Although Revelation 20:1-3, 7 makes reference to a thousand-year period when Satan will be bound, the concept of the "rapture" is based on a misinterpretation of 1 Thessalonians 4:16-17 KJV:

> "For the Lord himself shall descend from heaven with a shout, with the voice of the archangel, and with the trumpet of God: and the dead in Christ shall rise first: Then we which are alive and remain shall be caught up together with them in the clouds, to meet the Lord in the air: and so, shall we ever be with the Lord."

Some Protestant denominations, particularly those which tend to be fundamentalist in nature, have very carefully worked out theories about what will happen at the end of time and/or at Christ's second coming. The second coming of Christ is what we Catholics refer to as the parousia; which is the Greek word for "presence" or "arrival". Depending upon which group one is talking with, the "rapture" will take place at the beginning of Jesus' thousand-year (millennium) reign, and they will reign with Him; while others hold that the "rapture" will take place at the end of the thousand-year reign and will be followed immediately by the end of the world and the general judgement. There are even some who hold that the "rapture" will take place during the thousand-year reign. This has been a cause of great division among the various fundamentalist groups but is of little interest to Catholics. As Catholics, we focus our attention on the condition of the individual soul at the time of death rather than speculating on the timing of Jesus' parousia.

To understand 1 Thessalonians 4:16-17, we must look to the background of why St. Paul is writing this letter. St. Paul has had to leave Thessalonica hurriedly (Acts 17:10), leaving their religious instruction incomplete. One of the questions which had not been answered was whether the dead would be at any disadvantage in respect to the living when the Parousia of the Lord came. St. Paul's answer is in these verses of 1 Thessalonians, and it is to the effect that no one will have an advantage; when the Parousia comes, the living and the dead will meet Jesus together in their glorified bodies ("in the air" since they and their bodies have been changed from being corruptible to being incorruptible and they have become immortal rather than mortal).

Rather than concern ourselves about the timing of such things as the "rapture" or the parousia, we should read the verses in 1 Thessalonians which follow the ones just quoted:

> "Therefore encourage each other with these words. Now, brothers and sisters, about times and dates we do not need to write to you, for you know very well that the day of the Lord will come like a thief in the night. While people are saying, 'Peace and safety,' destruction will come on them suddenly, as labor pains on a pregnant woman, and they will not escape." (1 Thessalonians 4:18-5:3 NIV).

We must concern ourselves with living as if every day and hour may be our last on earth; so that we may be prepared to meet the divine Judge and be deemed worthy of enjoying eternity with Him.

Recommended Reading:

"Are You Pre, Mid, or Post?", A Catholic Answers Tracts, Catholic Answers, P. O. Box 17490, San Diego, CA 92177.

The Navarre Bible: Thessalonians and Pastoral Epistles, Four Courts Press, Blackrock, Co. Dublin, Ireland, 1992, pp. 49-50.

Keating, Karl, *Catholicism and Fundamentalism,* Ignatius Press, San Francisco, CA, 1988, pp. 19, 22.

Currie, David B., *Born Fundamentalist, Born Again Catholic,* Ignatius Press, San Francisco, CA, 1996, pp. 179-194.

Drummey, James J., *Catholic Replies,* C. R. Publications, Norwood, MA 02062, 1995, p. 171.

Q. What do Catholics believe about being reunited with their relatives in heaven?

A. No one knows exactly what heaven will be like, but Holy Scripture and Church teaching do give us some idea of the great joy which awaits us. What we do know is that:

> "What no eye has seen, what no ear has heard, and what no human mind conceived – the things God has prepared for those who love him." (1 Corinthians 2:9 and Isaiah 64:4 NIV).

The greatest joy of all will be our ability to see God Himself as He really is.

> "Now we see only a reflection as in a mirror; then we shall see face to face. Now I know in part: then I shall know fully, even as I am fully known." (1 Corinthians 13:12 NIV).

We will also be able to enjoy the company of Jesus in His humanity, with Mary His (and our) mother, Saints Peter and Paul, and with all the saints in heaven; including those of our personal families who have been judged worthy.

<u>Recommended Reading:</u>

Catechism of the Catholic Church, Libreria Editrice Vaticana, 1994, paras. 1023-1029.

Drummey, James J., *Catholic Replies,* C. R. Publications, Norwood, MA 02062, 1995, pp. 177-178.

MARY

Many non-Catholic Christians do not understand what Catholics believe about Mary and why. As a result, Catholic Marian beliefs have become a focal point in questions about the Catholic Church. If it can be shown that even one Marian belief is not true, then the Catholic claim of infallible teaching is wrong.

Q. My friends want to know and don't understand why we worship Mary and place her as high as God.
Q. Do Catholics worship Mary above Jesus?
Q. Do Catholics worship Mary?

A. To non-Catholics, the honor shown to Mary appears to be nothing other than the worship of Mary. This would place Mary on a level with God and be a violation of the First Commandment. Some non-Catholics have even gone so far as to coin the word "Mariolatry" for the Catholic devotion given to Mary. In fact, Catholic worship is reserved only for God. The Catholic Church even has special words for all this: "latria" is the worship offered and due to God alone, and "dulia" is the veneration given to the saints, including Mary. "Hyperdulia", more than "dulia", but far less than "latria" is the term applied to the honor given to Mary. The words "latria", "dulia" and "hyperdulia" can be confusing to the layperson, however, because we don't commonly use them even though they come from the New Testament Greek. They can appear to be nothing but smoke-and-minors to the non-Catholic who has never heard of them before.

The first question puts this whole area of discussion in perspective. Protestants, in their worship services, offer songs and praise and prayer to God; this is their highest form of worship. Since they don't have a priesthood, they have nothing else they can offer. Catholics on the other hand, offer the Sacrifice of the Mass to God. Our offering of sacrifice is made only to God and is our form of worship. This allows us to give lesser things such as songs and praise and prayer to those who can pray in our behalf before God, the saints and especially the Blessed Virgin Mary. When the Protestants see us offering what is their highest form of worship to someone other than God, it appears to them that we are worshiping someone other than God.

Why all this special attention given to Mary? Because she is Jesus' mother, the person who gave Him all His genetically human characteristics. Normally, a person gets their genetic characteristics from both the father and the mother but in the case of Jesus there was no human father to provide the genes which would be combined with Mary's. Mary is honored because God honored her by choosing her to be the mother of Jesus. All Catholic doctrines concerning Mary are related to and emerge from our understanding of her Son. Mary has no significance apart from Jesus. Mary says in Holy Scripture:

> "...from henceforth all generations shall call me blessed." (Luke 1:48 KJV).

Finally, let's look at Mary from Jesus' perspective. Jesus was a Hebrew; a perfect Hebrew who kept all the feasts, worshiped in the Temple, and most importantly, kept the commandments. This would have included the commandment to "honor thy father and thy mother" (Exodus 20:12; Deuteronomy 5:16). In Hebrew, the word "honor" means "glorify." Jesus would have glorified not only His Father, but as the perfect Hebrew, He would have honored His mother as well. When a Catholic gives honor to Mary, they are imitating Jesus. After all, Holy Scripture tells us:

> Follow God's example. (Ephesians 5:1 NIV);
>
> You became imitators of us and of the Lord. (1 Thessalonians 1:6 NIV).

Recommended Reading:

Catechism of the Catholic Church, Libreria Editrice Vaticana, 1994, paras. 971, 2096-2097, 2683-2684.

Keating, Karl, *Catholicism and Fundamentalism,* Ignatius Press, San Francisco, CA, 1988, pp. 280-281.

Schreck, Alan, *Catholic and Christian,* Servant Books, Ann Arbor, MI, 48107, 1984, pp. 163-189.

Currie, David B., *Born Fundamentalist, Born Again Catholic,* Ignatius Press, San Francisco, CA, 1996, pp. 155-177.

Roberts, Fr. Kenneth J., *Up on The Mountain,* Paraclete Press, Orleans, MA, 1992, pp. 69-97.

Rumble, Rev. Dr. Leslie & Carty, Rev. Charles Mortimer, *Radio Replies, Second Volume,* TAN Books & Publishers, Rockford, IL 61105, 1979, paras. 668-674.

Q. Why do Catholics have to have Mary to intercede for us when we pray?

A. Catholics do not "have to have" Mary to intercede for us. We can, and do, pray directly to God. However, we also recognize that having someone provide intercessory prayer for us is very beneficial. Few people feel uncomfortable about asking their friend or neighbor to pray for them, especially in time of need; after all, two prayers are better than one. Mary is, and always will be, the mother of Jesus. As a mother, she has certain rights and privileges, and this is why we ask her to intercede for us. Every prayer addressed to Mary is in reality a prayer asking a favor from God.

Recommended Reading:

Catechism of the Catholic Church, Libreria Editrice Vaticana, 1994, paras. 969, 975.

Rumble, Rev. Dr. Leslie & Carty, Rev. Charles Mortimer, *Radio Replies, First Volume,* TAN Books & Publishers, Rockford, IL 61105, 1979, paras. 1408-1416.

Rumble, Rev. Dr. Leslie & Carty, Rev. Charles Mortimer, *Radio Replies, Third Volume,* TAN Books & Publishers, Rockford, IL 61105, 1979, paras. 1321-1328.

Q. Why call Mary the "Mother of God"?

A. Because that is who she is. The title "Mother of God" was first formally applied to Mary by the Church at the Council of Ephesus in 431 A.D. This council was the 3rd Ecumenical Council of the Church. An ecumenical council is a general meeting of all the bishops of the Church whose (the council's) works are approved by a pope. The Council of Ephesus was called to answer the heresy of Nestorianism (which denied that Jesus was a person who was both fully divine and fully human), and the heresy of Pelagianism (which held that man could earn his own salvation through his natural powers). Pope Celestine I approved the works of this council.

The New Testament is the fulfillment of the Old Testament. In this regard, Abraham is called the father of all believers because he is the first to have unconditionally said "yes" to God throughout his life and willingly offered his son as sacrifice.

Likewise, Mary is called the mother of all believers because she is the first to have unconditionally said "yes" to God and bore Him the Son who was sacrificed for us all. God chose Mary to be the mother of His Son (Luke 1:31-32). Without the assent of this human woman, the birth of Jesus would not have taken place.

Jesus has God as His Father and Mary as His mother. Because she is Jesus' mother, the one who gave birth to Him, and because Jesus is God (one person both fully human and fully divine), Mary is called the "Mother of God".

All of this said, the title "Mother of God" is not without Biblical basis. In Holy Scripture it is recorded that Elizabeth says to Mary:

> "'But why am I so favored, that the mother of my Lord should come to me.'" (Luke 1:43 NIV).

"Lord" was a common name for God among the Old Testament Jews and the Jews of Jesus' time. For example, Jesus in Matthew 4:7 NIV says,

> "'Do not put the Lord your God to the test.'";

and in Luke 1:6 NIV, it is said of Zechariah and Elizabeth,

> "Both of them were righteous in the sight of God, observing all the Lord's commandments and regulations blamelessly."

In fact, every occurrence of "Lord" in Luke Chapter 1 is a direct reference to God. Elizabeth is actually addressing Mary as the "Mother of my God."

Many people today are disturbed by the title "Mother of God" although they have no problem with the title "Mother of Jesus." They then portray Mary as giving birth only to the human nature of Jesus. The problem with this approach is that Jesus is a person who possesses concurrently both human and divine natures. To ascribe only one nature would be a return to the Nestorian heresy. Mary gave birth to a person who was not a schizophrenic, sometimes human and sometimes divine, but fully human and divine at the same time. The natures cannot be separated. Mary gave birth to the Second Person of the Blessed Trinity, Who is God.

Recommended Reading:

Catechism of the Catholic Church, Libreria Editrice Vaticana, 1994, paras. 466, 495, 2677.

Mateo, Father, *Refuting the Attack on Mary: A Defense of Marian Doctrines,* Catholic Answers, San Diego, CA 92177, undated.

Fox, Father Robert J., *Protestant Fundamentalism and the Born Again Catholic,* Fatima Family Apostolate, Alexandria, SD 57311, 1991, pp. 157-187.

Q. How do you know that Mary is not Satan's helper to get people away from God?

A. It is assumed that the person asking this question is not questioning Mary's role in bringing Jesus into being on earth, but instead, is questioning the reported Marian apparitions since that time. The best way to resolve this question is to look at the test which Jesus Himself gave us. In Holy Scripture Jesus says:

> "Beware of false prophets, which come to you in sheep's clothing, but inwardly they are ravening wolves. Ye shall know them by their fruits." (Matthew 7:15-16 KJV).

Likewise, St. John tells us:

> "Beloved, believe not every spirit but try the spirits whether they are of God: because many false prophets are gone out into the world. Hereby know ye the Spirit of God: Every spirit that confesseth that Jesus Christ is come in the flesh is of God." (1 John 4:1-2 KJV).

All the approved Marian apparitions have the common themes of: amend your life; pray; make reparation for your sins; turn to Jesus for consolation. These are all good fruits and are from God.

All this said, no Catholic is required to believe any of the Marian apparitions. The Church has approved only a few of the reported apparitions of Mary such as those at Fatima in Portugal, Lourdes in France, Beauraing in Belgium, Akita in Japan, and Betania in Venezuela. Catholics are obligated as an article of faith to accept all public (or general) revelation. All public revelation ceased with the death of the last Apostle. All the Marian apparitions are private revelations and as such are binding only on the recipients. Approval simply means that the apparition does not teach things contrary to public revelation and is therefore worthy of belief.

<u>Recommended Reading:</u>

Keating, Karl, *What Catholics Really Believe - Setting the Record Straight,* Servant Publications, Ann Arbor, MI 48107, 1992, pp. 72-76.

Q. How can a virgin become a mother?

A. This is one of the mysteries of our faith. Even Mary and Joseph wondered how this could be:

> "'How will this be," Mary asked the angel, "since I am a virgin?'" (Luke 1:34 NIV);

> "Because Joseph her husband was faithful to the law, and yet did not want to expose her to public disgrace, he had in mind to divorce her quietly." (Matthew 1:19 NIV).

This is called a "mystery" because we cannot fully explain it. We know from Holy Scripture that the Holy Spirit came upon Mary and the power of the Most High overcame her (Luke 1:35). This is how Jesus was conceived rather than through the normal manner of sexual intercourse. The exact biology of what happened is unexplainable except as a miraculous intervention by God.

Mary's virgin birth is foretold in Genesis 3:15 KJV:

> "And I will put enmity between thee and the woman, and between thy seed and her seed; it shall bruise thy head, and thou shall bruise his heel."

Note that this is the only place in the Bible, and in fact in any of the writings of that time where "seed" (the Greek word is "spermatas") is attributed to a woman. In all other places, "seed" is considered to be a characteristic of the man. The virgin birth is also foretold in Isaiah 7:14 KJV:

> "Behold, a virgin shall conceive, and bear a son, and shall call his name Immanuel."

Q. Why believe Mary was forever virgin and sinless?

A. Both these beliefs have been held by the Church since the earliest times. In the case of Mary's perpetual virginity, this belief is based on Holy Scripture:

> "How shall this be, seeing I know not man?" (Luke 1:34 KJV).

Mary is not asking for instructions in sexual reproduction, she no doubt has a good idea of how babies are made. She is at this point in her life, married to Joseph although they do not yet live together. The Scriptures tell us that the angel said, "you will be with child (Luke 1:31)", not "you are with child." The angel is talking about a future event and the normal result of sexual relations in marriage after she and Joseph lived together would have been a child. Mary's statement in Luke 1:34 makes no sense unless there is a vow of life-long virginity involved, even in marriage.

The Ark of the Covenant in the Old Testament contained the word of God (the tablets containing the commandments). Likewise, Mary's womb was the Ark of the New Covenant.

Now let's look at the issue of Mary's sinless nature. Consider that when the angel addresses Mary at the Annunciation, the greeting is almost a name change:

> "Hail, thou that art highly favored, the Lord is with thee; blessed art thou among women." (Luke 1:28 KJV).

Mary (Miriam in Hebrew) means "beloved". In biblical times a person's name reflected what they were. Name changes have great theological significance in the Bible and this is almost as if her name is being changed from "beloved" to "thou that art highly favored". Since this is before Jesus has been conceived, to what is the angel referring? No doubt to her singular devotion to God, forsaking all earthly distractions and desecrations, and the fact that she had been conceived without sin in preparation for this event.

Being conceived without sin does not mean that Mary had no need of a redeemer. In fact, like every descendant of Adam, Mary had vital need of a redeemer. Mary's freedom from original sin was an unmerited gift of God in that she was redeemed by Christ at the moment of her conception. It is at the moment of conception that God creates the soul, and hers was created in a state of sanctifying grace. If you had the opportunity to create your mother, wouldn't you make her perfect in every way? This is why there are the doctrines of the perpetual virginity and Immaculate Conception of Blessed Virgin Mary.

Jesus refers to Mary's sinless nature when He addresses her as "woman" in John 2:4 and 19:26. Today, one looks at Him addressing her in this manner and thinks this is disrespectful or that He is admonishing her. In fact, Mary was not the first sinless woman, Adam's wife was also created sinless. When she was first created, Adam named her "woman (Genesis 2:23)". It was after the fall, when she was no longer sinless, that her name was changed to "Eve (Genesis 3:20)". By referring to Mary as "woman", Jesus is recognizing her sinless nature. As was said earlier, name changes in Holy Scripture are important.

Recommended Reading:

Catechism of the Catholic Church, Libreria Editrice Vaticana, 1994, paras. 411, 496-507, 510.

Ott, Dr. Ludwig, *Fundamentals of Catholic Dogma,* TAN Books and Publishers, Rockford, IL 61105, 1974, pp. 199-207.

Keating, Karl, *Catholicism and Fundamentalism,* Ignatius Press, San Francisco, CA, 94122, 1988, pp. 268-272, 282-289.

Currie, David B., *Born Fundamentalist, Born Again Catholic,* Ignatius Press, San Francisco, CA, 94122, 1996, pp. 155-177.

THE SAINTS AND ANGELS

Q. Why do you pray to saints?
Q. Why pray to saints?
Q. My friends don't understand praying to Saints. Why not pray directly to God?
Q. If Jesus said, "I am the way, the truth and the life No one can come to the Father except through me.", why then do we pray to Mary and the Saints?
Q. Why pray to angels?

A. First of all, we don't pray to saints but through them. Catholics can and do pray directly to God; the prayers of the Mass are directed to God the Father, Son, and Holy Spirit. Prayer to God is the most important thing we can do, but there is nothing wrong with asking the angels and saints to intercede with God in our behalf. After all, the angels witnessed the fall of one of their own (Satan) while they remained obedient to God and the saints faced the same problems and temptations that confront us and overcame them with lives of holiness. No Christian hesitates to ask their friends and neighbors to pray for their intentions and needs. The greatest friends we have are those who are in heaven cheering us on as we struggle to overcome our sinful nature and live the Christian life.

All through the Old Testament there are examples of people (Abraham, Moses, the prophets) praying for the benefit of others;

and of honor given to angels (Joshua 5:13-14; Daniel 8:17). In the New Testament we read"

> "The prayer of a righteous person is powerful and effective." (James 5:16 NIV).

Who is more righteous than one who has achieved their place in heaven? Just because some has ceased his or her earthly life doesn't mean that they are beyond our reach, or that they have ceased caring for us. The saints are alive in heaven as 1 Corinthians 15:22 tells us, and Revelation 5:8 tells us that the prayers of the saints are offered to God. The saints are God's masterpieces and what artist would say, "Don't look at my works, pay attention only to me?" We give honor to God by praising His accomplishments.

When Jesus established His Church, He didn't establish one Church on earth and another unrelated Church in heaven. This is why, when we recite the Apostles' Creed or the Nicene Creed (the Profession of Faith) in Mass, we say that "we believe in the communion of saints"; we are all part of one spiritual community, God's family. As family, we care about what happens to one another. When Jesus was asked what was the greatest commandment, He replied that the first was to love God, and the second was to love our neighbor. The saints in heaven keep this second commandment by interceding for us and helping us to love God. We are all alive in Christ (1 Corinthians 15:22), and since we affirm the resurrection of the dead, asking the saints for assistance should pose no problem. (See Apostles' Creed in Appendix.)

Jesus is the way, the truth, and the life. He is the only pathway linking heaven and earth. The saints are ones who have lived the Christian life and received their eternal reward; they have walked in Jesus' footsteps. We ask that by their example and assistance, that we may walk in those footsteps as well. We do not pray to the saints to avoid Jesus who is the way, the truth, and the life, but we do ask for additional assistance in directing our needs through Jesus to God the Father.

Recommended Reading:

Catechism of the Catholic Church, Libreria Editrice Vaticana, 1994, paras. 946, 954-959, 2674-2679, 2683-2684, 2692.

Keating, Karl, *Catholicism and Fundamentalism,* Ignatius Press, San Francisco, CA 94122, 1988, pp. 259-267.

Mbukanma, Rev. Jude O., *Is it in the Bible?,* Scripture Keys Ministries Australia, Broadford, Victoria, Australia, 1987, pp. 8-9.

Q. Why do you have statues to pray to?
Q. Why do Catholics pray to statues?
Q. Isn't it a sin to kneel before statues and icons?
Q. How do we answer those who criticize us for worshiping idols?

A. The use of statues, icons, pictures, and even stained-glass windows have their origins in the Old Testament. Statues are nothing more than three-dimensional pictures, while icons and stained-glass windows are two-dimensional pictures. No one feels uncomfortable carrying a picture of a loved one in their wallet or displaying their photo or portrait in a prominent place in their home; these pictures remind the viewer of the person depicted. So, it is with statues, icons and pictures of the saints; they remind us of the person depicted and the honor which they bestowed upon God.

The use of all images in worship of God is not forbidden by the first commandment (second commandment as the Protestants number them). Exodus 20:4-5 NIV says:

> "You shall not make for yourself an image in the form of anything in heaven above or on the earth beneath or in the waters below. You shall not bow down to them or worship them; for I, the Lord your God, am a jealous God."

The prohibition here is not the manufacture of images (pictures), but the worship of the images instead of God. This may be more clearly seen five chapters later where God commands the Israelites through Moses to:

> "... make two cherubim out of hammered gold at the ends of the cover [of the Ark of the Covenant]." (Exodus 25:18 NIV).

Cherubim are angels; something in heaven above. Then God commands them to make an image of something on the earth:

> "Make a lamp stand of pure gold. Hammer out its base and shaft and make its flowerlike cups, buds and blossoms ... Three cups shaped like almond flowers with buds and blossoms..." (Exodus 25:31-36 NIV).

The Israelites would kneel before these images as part of their Temple worship; not in worship of the images but in worship of God.

All Christians, Protestant and Catholic, use a symbol of a fish to depict Jesus. The fish is something in the waters below.

When one sees a person kneeling in prayer before a statue, this doesn't mean that the person is worshiping the statue (or the person depicted by the statue). Worship is given only to God. Honor and praise are given to the saints for the example and assistance they have provided in our quest to do God's will. As was noted in the chapter titled "MARY", "Protestants, in their worship services, offer songs and praise and prayer to God; this is their highest form of worship. Since they don't have a priesthood, they have nothing else they can offer. Catholics on the other hand, offer the Sacrifice of the Mass to God. Our offering of sacrifice is made only to God and is our form of worship. This allows us to give lesser things such as songs and praise and prayer to those who can pray in our behalf before God: the saints and especially the Blessed Virgin Mary. When the Protestants see us offering what is their highest form of worship to someone other than God, it appears to them that we are worshiping someone other than God."

As can be seen, the use of images has Old Testament origins where it is ordered by God; not as objects of worship, but as objects used in the worship of God. Statues, icons, and stained-glass windows became popular in the early church as the people had no Bibles (printing hadn't been invented yet) and even if they had been able to possess them, the average Christian couldn't read. The images told the Bible stories and were used as methods of evangelization and instruction.

Recommended Reading:

Mbukanma, Rev. Jude O., *Is it in the Bible?*, Scripture Keys Ministries Australia, Broadford, Victoria, Australia, 1987, pp. 2-4.

Q. Why so many saints?

A. There are billions and billions of saints that we don't know of yet. When we think of Saints today, we think of people whose lives are notable for their holiness and heroic virtue. St. Paul, in his letter to the Colossians (1:2 KJV) uses the term "saint" for Christians in general. Bestowal of the title of "Saint" by the Church declares that these people are in heaven and may be publicly invoked for devotion. There is no doubt that there are many saints in heaven who have not been declared saints. It has been said that while we are all "saints", we must continue striving all our earthly life for a share in His life and glory.

Recommended Reading:

Stravinskas, Rev. Peter M. J., *Our Sunday Visitors Catholic Encyclopedia,* Our Sunday Visitor, Huntington, IN 46750, 1991, pp. 860-861.

Q. Who was the first person to canonized a saint?

A. The first to be canonized a saint by a pope was Saint Ulrich by Pope John XV in the year 993. Prior to that time, communities of devotion developed around certain holy individuals, particularly martyrs, and these communities grew until the persons were declared Saints by popular acclamation.

Q. Who has given the greatest contribution to the Church and what was it?

A. The greatest contribution was given to the Church by Jesus, who gave His life in order to establish it. Next in line after Jesus is the Blessed Virgin Mary who gave us Jesus. Then there are the martyrs, who gave their lives rather than profane or deny it.

Q. Why do we have novenas to different Saints?

A. A novena is the praying of a formula prayer for personal devotion. The prayer is said for nine consecutive days or once a week for nine weeks. Most often these prayers are for a personal intention and are in honor of a particular saint (who may have overcome a similar problem) or an aspect of Christ Himself; for example, Sacred Heart. Although the practice of praying novenas didn't come about until the 17th century, the number nine is taken from the nine days that Mary, the Apostles, and the other disciples spent praying in the Upper Room between the Ascension and the coming of the Holy Spirit on Pentecost (Acts 1:12-14).

Q. What good are all the medals and statues you have?

A. The medals and statues are just reminders of the persons they represent. When we see them, we are reminded of God's grace and our attention is focused on God. The statues and medals serve only to remind us to pray to God for the strength and perseverance to be like those who have gone before us to be with Him.

Q. Why are some angels, like St. Michael, considered Saints and others are just angels? People think that only humans can be Saints.

A. It is true that normally we think only of humans becoming Saints. According to the dictionary, the word "saint" is derived from the Latin "sanctus", which means holy or sacred. An angel is a purely spiritual being and as such is noted for being holy. Heaven is the place where the angels who surround God live, along with the saints. The three angels which we refer to as "Saints" are the only three who are named in Holy Scripture. Michael remained faithful to God and led the victory against the fallen angels (Revelation 12:7-9). Gabriel announced to the Blessed Virgin Mary that she was to bear the Son of God (Luke 1:26-38). Raphael identified himself as one of the seven holy angels who present the prayers of the saints and enter into the presence of the glory of the Holy One (Tobit, 12:15, RSV-CE). They are referred to as Saints because they are holy, they dwell with God, and they have a name to which we can add the title of "Saint".

Recommended Reading:

Catechism of the Catholic Church, Libreria Editrice Vaticana, 1994, para. 326.

Q. Do people become angels when they die?

A. No. Angels are purely spiritual beings who were created by God with an intellect and a free will. People were separately created by God and are physical beings with a spiritual soul and who also have an intellect and a free will. When we die, if we die with no mortal sin on our soul, our soul goes to heaven to be with God forever. and this is where we await the General Judgement when we will be reunited with our glorified body. Angels have never had a body with which to be reunited.

Recommended Reading:

Catechism of the Catholic Church, Libreria Editrice Vaticana, 1994, para. 1023.

Q. Did St. Patrick raise people from the dead?

A. Saint Patrick, patron saint of Ireland and Nigeria, is believed to have died and been buried in or about the year 461. Recorded details from that time are scarce, especially since the Church in Ireland was under persecution for centuries, including the time of Saint Patrick. Biographers in later years have written many things which, when compared with one another, appear muddled, mythical, and even contradictory. The details of his life in Ireland are uncertain.

THE ROSARY

Q. What is the rosary? Why do Catholics pray the Rosary?

A. The rosary is a type of meditative prayer focused on the events in the life of Our Lord and the Blessed Virgin Mary. The rosary was popularized by St. Dominic (1170-1221) who is said to have received it from the Blessed Virgin Mary to combat the Albigensian heresy, which taught that all matter, including the body, was created by evil, while the spirit was created by God.

During medieval times monks had adopted the practice of daily praying the 150 Psalms, the Psalms being divided into three sets of 50 each. Since many of the lay brothers of these orders were illiterate and couldn't read the Psalms, the practice arose of reciting the Our Father 150 times. This became the "poor man's breviary". This practice spread to the laity and as time went on other easily remembered prayers were added. During the fifteenth and sixteenth centuries the Rosary settled into its present form starting with the Apostles' Creed, the Our Father, the Hail Mary, and the Glory Be then 15 sets of 10 Hail Mary's, called mysteries, while meditating on the lives of Jesus and Mary; Joyful, Sorrowful, Glorious Mysteries. The Luminous Mysteries were added in 2002 by Pope John Paul II. The Rosary is not just a Catholic prayer; many members of other denominations also pray this meditative prayer, especially Episcopalians and Lutherans. (See Apostles' Creed in the Appendix.)

Recommended Reading:

Catechism of the Catholic Church, Libreria Editrice Vaticana, 1994, paras. 2678, 2708.

Meagher, Paul K. OP, O'Brien, Thomas C. & Aherne, Sister Consuelo M. SSJ, *Encyclopedic Dictionary of Religion,* Corpus Publications, Washington, D.C., 1979, pp. 3091-3092.

Drummey, James J., *Catholic Replies,* C. R. Publications, Norwood, MA 02062, 1995, p. 138.

Q. What are the Rosary beads used for?
Q. Why do we pray with beads to the Blessed Mother?
Q. What is the significance of ten Hail Mary's per decade of the Rosary?

A. The word "bead" derives from the Middle English "bede" which originally meant "prayer". The beads of the rosary are used to keep track of the prayers. Early beads were nothing but pebbles which were transferred from one pocket to another. As presently configured, the Our Father is prayed on the solitary beads that separate the groups of ten beads (the decades), the Hail Mary is prayed on each of the ten beads of the decade, then the Glory Be is prayed on the solitary bead separating the decades; the whole process is then repeated. A set of fifty Hail Mary's, with the accompanying Our Father's and Glory Be's, constitutes one circuit of the beads on most rosary sets today. As each decade (ten Hail Mary's) is recited, the person meditates upon one of the events of Jesus' and Mary's life; so that upon completing one circuit of the beads, five events have been contemplated and fifty Psalms (represented by the Hail Mary's) have been honored.

A quick look at the construction of the Hail Mary discloses that although it is addressed to Mary, the focus is prayer to God (parenthetical words are insertions into the scriptural reference, where applicable). "Hail (Mary), full of grace, the Lord is with you" is the greeting of the angel Gabriel at the Annunciation (Luke 1:28). "Blessed are you among women, and blessed is the fruit of your womb (Jesus)" is Elizabeth's greeting to Mary at the Visitation (Luke 1:42). "Holy Mary, Mother of God" addresses the person to whom we are speaking, using the title accorded her during the 5th century. This title is discussed in the chapter titled "MARY". "Pray for us" is a request for prayer to God which is no different from asking our neighbor to pray for us except that Mary is already in heaven. "Sinners now, and at the hour of our death" is an acknowledgment of our sinful status and the times when the prayer to God are requested in our behalf.

These are the two most important times in our lives: "Now", because we recognize our sinful nature and desire God's assistance to change it; "At the hour of our death", because then, we will be judged and will be most needful of God's mercy.

Recommended Reading:

Frazier, T. L., "The Rosary Dissected", *This Rock,* The Magazine of Catholic Apologetics & Evangelization, September 1994, pp. 16-20.

JESUS

Q. How do you know that Jesus is not St. Michael?

A. That Jesus was Michael the Archangel is a teaching of the Jehovah's Witnesses who deny the Trinity and that Jesus is God. The Witnesses base their belief on 1 Thessalonians 4:16 KJV:

> "For the Lord himself shall descend from heaven with a shout, with the voice of the archangel, and with the trumpet of God ..."

The Bible does tell us that St. Michael is an angel. Jude 9 KJV says:

> "Yet Michael the archangel, when contending with the devil ..."

This same Holy Bible also tells us that Jesus is both God and man:

> "...no man can say that Jesus is the Lord, but by the Holy Ghost." (1 Corinthians 12:3 KJV);

And also,

> "We see Jesus, who was made a little lower than the angels for the suffering of death, crowned with glory and honor; that he by the grace of God should taste death for every man." (Hebrews 2:9 KJV).

"Lord" is a term used for God in the Hebrew language. At the same time, He was "made a little lower than the angels"; He became man. We have here the hierarchy of God, angels, man.

In the account of Jesus' baptism by John the Baptist, God says of Jesus:

> "This is my beloved Son, in whom I am well pleased." (Matthew 3:17 KJV).

While in Hebrews 1:5-6 KJV we read:

> "For unto what of the angels said he at any time, 'Thou art my Son this day have I begotten thee'? And again, 'I will be to him a father, and he shall be to me a son'? And again, when he bringeth in the firstbegotten into the world, he saith, and let all the angels of God worship him."

If God calls Jesus, "Son" but doesn't call any of the angels "Son" and at the same time directs the angels to worship Jesus when He is walking upon this earth, it is quite obvious that Jesus was not St. Michael, the Archangel, but is in fact God incarnate.

Q. Was Jesus an only child?
Q. How do you know that Mary had no other children?
Q. What tells us that Jesus doesn't have any brothers?
Q. Doesn't the Bible teach that Jesus had siblings?

A. There are some who claim that Jesus was not an only child and that Mary had children in addition to Jesus. Whether Jesus was an only child or whether He had a dozen siblings really matters not a whit to them except that it attacks the Catholic Church in what they consider to be the weak area, Marian doctrine. They will cite such biblical passages as:

> "...his mother and his brethren stood without..." (Matthew 12:46 KJV);

> "Is not this the carpenter, the son of Mary, the brother of James, and Joses and of Juda, and Simon? and are not his sisters here with us?" (Mark 6:3 KJV);

> "For even his own brothers did not believe in him." (John 7:5 NIV);

> "... with the women, and Mary the mother of Jesus, and with his brethren." (Acts 1:14 KJV);

And

> "…the brethren of the Lord …" (1 Corinthians 9:5 NIV);

or

> "And knew her not till she brought forth her firstborn son." (Matthew 1:25 NIV).

The Church teaches us that Mary was perpetually a virgin and this is what we affirm every time we recite the Confiteor (Penitential Rite), "… and I ask the blessed Mary, ever virgin …" The perpetual virginity of Mary has been defended by the Church since the 4th century when St. Athanasius wrote in his Discourses Against the Aryans (358-362 A.D.): "He took true human flesh from the Ever-Virgin Mary." Pope St. Siricius defended the teaching in 392 A.D., and the fifth ecumenical council (Constantinople 11) in 553 A.D. gave Mary the title "Perpetual Virgin."

Why the difference? It comes with the fact that almost twenty-one centuries have passed since the books of the Bible were written and customs have changed, along with the fact that some people read into the texts meanings which were not intended. First century customs cannot be interpreted with twenty-first century values.

In the first case, what was the custom for calling someone your brother, sister, or using the collective term of brethren? In Genesis 14:14 (KJV), Lot is called Abraham's brother but Genesis 11:27 tells us that Lot was the son of Haran, Abraham's brother. This shows that the terms were used to include cousins; but these terms were not even limited to close relatives. Why was this? Neither Hebrew nor Aramaic (the language spoken by Jesus and the Apostles) had a special word for cousin. Instead, the words brother, sister, brethren were commonly used. The writers of the New Testament, although writing in Greek, were raised in the Hebrew tradition and kept to this tradition as they were writing primarily to other Jewish Christians. Acts 2:46 illustrates that these Jewish Christians went to temple in addition to worshiping together.

Now, let's go back to Mark 6:3 where the "brothers" of Jesus are named and consider James and Joses. Compare the descriptions of the women at the foot of the cross in Matthew 27:56, Mark 15:40 and John 19:25. From this we find that Mary the mother of James and Joses must be the wife of Cleophas. No one has ever suggested that the Blessed Virgin remarried, especially since Jesus entrusted her care to John. Similar arguments can be made for the other 'brethren'.

Let's go on to Matthew 1:25 and find the meaning of "until" (or "till", or "unto", or "to" in some translations). "He knew her not till she brought forth her firstborn son", doesn't necessarily mean that he knew her after the event took place. For example, in 2 Samuel 6:23 we find the verse that Michal, the daughter of Saul, had no children to (or unto) the day of her death. Does this mean that she had children after she died? Jesus said,

> "And surely I am with you always, to the very end of the age." (Matthew 28:19-20 NIV).

Jesus surely does not mean He will not be with us after the end of the age.

Sometimes someone will assert that since Jesus is referred to as the "firstborn", others must have followed. This shows a misunderstanding of the use of the term. Under Mosaic law, the "firstborn" son was to be sanctified (Exodus 34:20). This doesn't mean that the parents had to wait until a second son was born. The first boy born was termed "firstborn" (the one who opened the womb) even if he was an only child.

Finally, let's look at the Annunciation itself in Luke 1:28-34. Mary's response, "How shall this be, seeing I know not a man?", makes no sense unless she had taken a vow to remain perpetually a virgin. At this point in her life, Mary is betrothed, which is by Jewish custom, married to Joseph; although they have not yet taken up residence together, an event that took place after the marriage feast. The angel Gabriel has just told her that she will have a son, not that she is already pregnant. If she were planning to have relations with Joseph after the marriage feast, the likely result would be a child. Only if she had taken a vow of perpetual virginity does her response make sense. Some say that such a vow would result in an "unnatural" marriage. Is it "natural" to have a true virgin give birth? Is it "natural" to have angels announce the birth of your child? Is it "natural" to raise the Son of God in your family? All these events are "supernatural".

Was Jesus an only child? In the biological sense, yes. In the spiritual sense, Romans 8:15-17 tells us that we are adopted children of God and coheirs with Christ if only we suffer with Him. Malachi 2:10 KJV says:

"Have we not all one father? Hath not one God created us?".

Suffice it to say that Jesus has millions of "brethren".

Recommended Reading:

Catechism of the Catholic Church, Libreria Editrice Vaticana, 1994, paras. 496-507, 510.

Keating, Karl, *Catholicism and Fundamentalism,* Ignatius Press, San Francisco, CA, 1988, pp. 282-289.

"Brethren of the Lord", A Catholic Answers Tracts, Catholic Answers, P. O. Box 17490, San Diego, CA 92177.

"Does Greek prove Jesus had Brothers?", *This Rock,* The Magazine of Catholic Apologetics and Evangelization, May/June 1992, p. 54.

"Keeping up with the Jameses?", *This Rock,* The Magazine of Catholic Apologetics and Evangelization, October 1992, p. 29.

PRACTICES

Q. Why do we as Catholics have to take part in crucifying Jesus (saying the Passion)? I know that it is just so that we as humans can see what Jesus did for us, but to me it's like crucifying Our Lord all over again. It hurts me to see everybody taking part in My Lord's (and Our Lord's) crucifixion.

A. Jesus does not suffer and die all over again. His passion, death and resurrection, were once for all persons and for all time. Each and every Mass however does make this event present for us as we re-present (as opposed to represent) His Sacrifice to the Father. In the Sacrifice of the Mass, we join Jesus at the Last Supper and accompany Him to Calvary as He makes His Perfect Sacrificial Offering to God the Father in our behalf. As the passion narrative is read every Passion (Palm) Sunday and Good Friday, the parishioners take part in the reading so that they will be reminded of just how much Jesus gave to us and that we are to walk in His footsteps with the same diligence and determination. This is not a sad recalling of events but a joyful recounting. After all, if it had not been for His sacrifice, heaven would not have been opened for us. As God, Jesus knew the happiness of heaven by eternal experience; He also foreknew the further secondary happiness awaiting Him in His risen humanity. He did not desire to remain on earth any longer than He did, but the knowledge of His happier state in heaven didn't free Him from the natural dread of the means by which He was to attain it. The conformity of His human will to the Divine Will as to the time and manner of His death is the truly meritorious event which is celebrated.

Recommended Reading:

Catechism of the Catholic Church, Libreria Editrice Vaticana, 1994, paras. 571-573, 599-623

Rumble, Rev. Dr. Leslie & Carty, Rev. Charles Mortimer, *Radio Replies, Third Volume,* TAN Books & Publishers, Rockford, IL 611051, 1979, paras. 727-735.

Q. Why can't you eat meat on Fridays during Lent?

Q. During Lent we do not eat meat on Fridays. Isn't fish considered meat?

Q. Why do you give up stuff for Lent?

A. The practice of abstinence (doing without certain things) goes back to the Old Testament and the Jewish dietary laws which were carried over into parts of the early Christian church until the Council of Jerusalem (Acts 15). The theological reasoning is that it is a method of atoning for sin since chastising the body brings it under control of the spirit. Abstinence is first mentioned in a Church document in a decree of the Council of Toledo in the year 447 A.D. where the custom was to abstain primarily from meat on all Fridays and on days of penance. Canon 1251 of the *1983 Code of Canon Law* prescribes "abstinence from meat, or from some other food as decided upon by the Episcopal Conference (conference of bishops) on all Fridays, unless a solemnity should fall on a Friday. Abstinence and fasting are to be observed on Ash Wednesday and Good Friday." The National Conference of Catholic Bishops of the United States (USCCB) made abstinence from meat mandatory on Ash Wednesday and all Fridays of Lent and recommended that it be observed on all Fridays of the year but has allowed individual Catholics to substitute another penance on Fridays if they could not abstain from meat. For purposes of abstinence, fish is not considered to be meat because it comes from a cold-blooded animal rather than a warm-blooded one. Secondarily, early Christian art and literature used fish as a symbol of the Eucharist because the Greek word for fish, "ichthus", is an acrostic (the first letters from the word) for "Jesus Christ, Son of God, Savior".

The 40 days of Lent (Sundays are excluded from the count since we celebrate the Resurrection of the Lord on this day) signify the change which we wish to make in our life. Throughout Holy Scripture, the number 40 signifies a time of change. During this time abstinence from something, whether it be sweets, coffee or TV is an offering to God and a method of prayer. Every time we are tempted by whatever we have decided to abstain from, we are to remind ourselves that we have given this up for God so that He can bring us closer to Himself.

Recommended reading:

Father Sheedy 's Ask Me A Question, Our Sunday Visitor, Huntington, IN 46750, 1989, pp. 15-16.

Q. Why do we give peace to each other?

Q. When we give the sign of peace, is it necessary to shake hands? Can't we just nod and say, "Peace be with you"? Some of us have arthritis, etc.

A. Initially called the kiss of peace, the origin of the sign of peace can be found in Romans 16:16 NIV:

> "Greet one another with a holy kiss.";

And also,

> "Peace I leave with you; my peace I give you. I do not give to you as the world gives. Do not let your hearts be troubled and do not be afraid." (John 14:27 NIV);

> "First go and be reconciled to your brother; then come and offer your gift." (Matthew 5:24 NIV).

St. Justin the Martyr, writing about 50 A.D., describes the Mass thus: "Having concluded the prayers, we greet one another with a kiss. Then there is brought to the president of the brethren bread and a cup of water and of watered wine. (First Apology, 65)"

As can be seen, the rite was incorporated into the liturgy in the very early Church. Over the years the location of the rite has been changed several times with different meanings. When it was before the Offertory (such as was described by St. Justin), it signified the desire to make peace with one another in the family of God; when it was moved to its present position after the Consecration, it became a declaration of love and unity.

No one is required to shake hands with anyone else; if shaking hands makes someone uncomfortable or is painful, a smile and a courteous bow while wishing your neighbor the peace of Christ is perfectly acceptable.

Recommended Reading:

Stravinskas, Rev. Peter M. J., *The Catholic Answer Book 2,* Our Sunday Visitor, Huntington, IN 46750, 1994, pp. 161, 169-170.

Drummey, James J., *Catholic Replies,* C. R. Publications, Norwood, MA 02062, 1995, pp. 301-303.

Father Sheedy 's Ask Me A Question, Our Sunday Visitor, Huntington, IN 46750, 1989, p. 212.

Q. Why do we sit, stand, kneel so much?

Q. Why is there so much kneeling during church?

A. Sitting is the posture of learning. The custom at the time of Jesus was for not only the students but the instructor to sit. Aside from the feeding of the 5,000 and the feeding of the 4,000 where the crowds were instructed to sit, Acts 8:31 tells of the instruction of the Ethiopian eunuch, and Mark 9:35, Luke 4:20-21, John 4:6, John 8:2 and Acts 16:13 all attest to this posture at the time of Jesus. This is why we sit for the first and second reading, and for the homily; we are at Mass to receive instruction in God's Word.

Standing is a posture of prayer, and it indicates a reverence for God. The custom at the time of Jesus was to stand while at prayer. Matthew 6:5 and Mark 11:25 attest to this posture. This is why, in the Mass today, when the priest says, "Let us pray", it is the clue for us to stand. Standing as a sign of reverence is shown when we stand for the entrance and recessional processions and for the reading of the Gospel. For the early Christians standing also took on a symbolic reference to the Resurrection of Christ. The early Christians frequently stood facing the East toward the rising sun, which was regarded as a symbol of Christ Himself as it illuminated their lives anew each day.

Kneeling is also a posture of reverence and prayer, especially supplication. This is attested to in Psalm 95:6 NIV:

> "Come, let us bow down in worship: let us kneel before the Lord our Maker."

Also, see the New Testament passages as Matthew 17:14, Mark 1:40, Acts 9:40, Romans 14:11, Ephesians 3:14 and Philippians 2:10. By kneeling, we express our humility before the greatness of God as we adore Him. This is why we kneel during the times of consecration and communion while at Mass. We also kneel when we pray fervently and as a sign of penance. By kneeling, Catholics are doing what Christians and Jews have long done. To reject this posture in worship is to reject the Holy Scriptures and our heritage. Strange as it may seem today, at one time the Church actually had to institute rules which limited the kneeling at Mass as it had become commonplace to kneel almost throughout the entire celebration.

Prostration as an expression of humility before the greatness of God is seldom seen anymore. Matthew 26:39 NIV,

"He fell with his face to the ground and prayed."

And Mark 14:35 shows Jesus in this posture at the Garden of Gethsemane. Prostration is prescribed primarily for episcopal and sacerdotal ordinations and at the beginning of the Good Friday Services (although kneeling is allowed in its stead at the Good Friday Services).

Recommended Reading:

Lang, Rev. Jovian P., *Dictionary of the Liturgy,* Catholic Book Publishing Company, New York, NY, 1989, pp. 512-513.

This Rock, The Magazine of Catholic Apologetics & Evangelization, September 1996, p. 44.

Q. Why doesn't the congregation wait to sit back down when the deacon is putting away the chalices after Communion?

A. We kneel as a sign of our respect for the real presence of Our Lord in the Eucharist. The rubrics of the Mass do not state when one should be seated after Communion. My feeling is that one should remain kneeling while the sacred vessels are being cleansed, no matter whether it is the priest or the deacon who is doing the cleansing. The storing of the vessels indicates that the cleansing has been completed and Our Lord is now in repose in the tabernacle.

Q. Why do we have a cross on the altar?

Q. Why do Catholics celebrate the death of Christ more so than the resurrection?

A. The General Instruction of the Roman Missal states, "There is also to be a cross, clearly visible to the congregation, either on the altar or near it (no. 117)." The Latin word translated as "cross" is crux which to Catholic Christians means the object carrying the body of our crucified Savior; what is also known as the crucifix, a cross with corpus attached.

The Catholic Church leaves the corpus on the cross not because we worship a dead Christ or celebrate the death of Christ more so than the Resurrection, but as a reminder of what He did in our behalf. It was through His death on the cross that we were redeemed. In Catholic spirituality, the cross and Resurrection are inseparable for Christ, and also for those who would be His disciples. To have the light of the Resurrection without the cross was impossible for Our Lord, and we are all called to follow in His footsteps. We are all told to pick up our cross and follow Him (Matthew 10:38; 16:24; Mark 8:34; Luke 9:23). Sacrifice, as we are reminded by the presence of the corpus, is what He did for us and is what we are called to do if we are to truly be His disciples.

> "The Spirit himself testifies with our spirit that we are God's children. Now if we are children, then we are heirs - heirs of God and co-heirs with Christ, if indeed we share in his sufferings in order that we may also share in his glory." (Romans 8:16-17 NIV).

It is His sacrifice on the cross which we re-present to the Father at each Mass as we join with Jesus in His eternal presentation of His sacrifice in heaven as was witnessed by Saint John:

> "Then I saw a Lamb, looking as if it had been slain, standing in the center of the throne." (Revelation 5:6 NIV).

In short, Jesus couldn't separate His crucifixion from His resurrection, and neither should we. In the words of Saint John and Saint Paul:

> "Just as Moses lifted up the snake in the desert, so the Son of Man must be lifted up, that everyone who believes may have eternal life in him," (John 3:14-15 NIV),

And also,

> "...but we preach Christ crucified: a stumbling block to the Jews and foolishness to Gentiles." (1 Corinthians 1:23 NIV).

<u>Recommended Reading</u>

Drummey, James J., *Catholic Replies,* C. R. Publications, Norwood, MA 02062, 1995, pp. 249-250.

Father Sheedy's Ask Me A Question, Our Sunday Visitor, Huntington, IN 46750, 1989, pp. 68-69.

Q. What is the significance of the striking of the chest during various periods of the Mass?

A. The striking of the chest is an ancient sign of sorrow and repentance which has been continued as part of our liturgical rite.

It is a gesture which is symbolic of the feeling of repentance: and the idea of humility. The striking of the chest occurs during the Penitential Rite ("I have sinned through my own fault") and in Eucharistic Prayer I at the words, "Though we are sinners." The striking is done with the right hand, with the left hand placed on the chest at a lower level. The basis in Holy Scripture for this practice can be found in Luke 18:13 NIV:

> "But the tax collector stood at a distance. He would not even look up to heaven, but beat his breast and said, 'God, have mercy on me, a sinner.'";

And in Luke 23:48 NIV at the death of Jesus,

> "When all the people who had gathered to witness this sight saw what took place, they beat their breasts and went away."

Q. Many of the church's decorative, ornamental pieces are beautiful. My question is this: Why if Jesus and His followers were of a simple life with meager surroundings and no personal belongings, does the Catholic Church have such an overabundance of gilded, ornamental objects?

A. A beautiful church with fine ornamental pieces and sacred vessels serve to remind us that we are actually in the presence of the Godhead. In Exodus 25:8-26:34, we are told that the Holy of Holies, where the glory cloud of God resided until the end of the first temple period, was lavishly furnished at God's direction with items of gold. Revelation 21:10-21 describes the heavenly Jerusalem in which we all hope to dwell one day; with its streets of gold, gates of pearl, and foundations decorated with every kind of precious stone.

Jesus, who you correctly recognize as not surrounding Himself with creature comforts, never takes issue with the decoration of His Father's house, but He does take issue with the desecration of it, with those who seek to make it common. Not all church buildings are ornately decorated. In mission countries they may be nothing more than a plain grass hut. The decorations you see come from the gifts of the parishioners whose desire is to honor God's house because they believe that nothing can be too good for God. Church buildings since the earliest times have been furnished with gilded and ornamental objects because they are God's dwelling place; He resides in the tabernacle once again. These decorations also serve to remind us of the glory which awaits us in heaven.

Q. Why with all its wealth doesn't the Church do more to help the poor?

A. The wealth of the Church to which you refer is primarily in the form of works of art and manuscripts; there is very little cold hard cash sitting around. In John 12:3-8, we are told of the woman who poured expensive perfume on Jesus' feet: A man objected, saying that it should have been sold and the money given to the poor, but Jesus praises her because she has given honor to Him. We all know that the man who objected was named Judas – the man who held the purse and stole from it, and the man who betrayed Jesus.

If all the works of art which are portable (this rules out such objects as the Sistine Chapel ceiling which are really part of the building) and all the manuscripts were sold, the cash realized would be less than what the United States spent in famine relief to Somalia during the United Nations effort. Then, most of these articles would no longer be available for public viewing or scholarly study and the poor would at best be minimally and only temporarily better off.

Through its various arms (organizations such as Catholic Relief, Catholic Charities, the Sisters of the Poor, the Knights of Columbus, and the Saint Vincent de Paul Society, to name but a few) the Catholic Church is the largest non-governmental provider of relief to the poor in the world.

Recommended Reading:

Rumble, Rev. Dr. Leslie & Carty, Rev. Charles Mortimer, *Radio Replies, Second Volume,* TAN Books & Publishers, Rockford, IL 61105, 1979, paras. 408-409, 1041-1045.

Q. How is it that the very young people do not know how to properly approach the altar and to properly conduct themselves after receiving Holy Communion? I have seen some very disturbing sights.

A. The primary teachers of children are the parents. One should not depend upon, or even expect, that proper conduct during Mass will be taught as part of the religious education program of any parish. By the time the children are old enough to be enrolled in a religious education class, they are old enough to have been taught how to sit still without talking, how to make the sign of the cross and how to genuflect. If they don't know this basic behavior, it takes valuable time away from the rest of the students while old habits are broken and new ones are learned.

If you are a parent and aren't sure of these basics yourself or have other questions, make an appointment with your pastor who will be more than glad to instruct you so you can instruct your child.

Recommended Reading:
Catechism of the Catholic Church, Libreria Editrice Vaticana, 1994, paras. 2224-2227.

Q. What is the Church's position on cremation for burial?

A. Canons 1176 and 1184 of the *1983 Code of Canon Law* states that no Catholic is to be deprived of the Church's funeral rites except the following, if they died unrepentant:

1. Notorious apostates, heretics and schismatics;
2. Those who chose cremation for reasons opposed to the faith;
3. Manifest public sinners whose funerals would give public scandal to the faithful.

The Church recommends the practice of burying the bodies of the dead because the body was once the temple of the Holy Spirit.

However, the Church does allow cremation provided it has not been chosen for reasons opposed to Christian faith such as hatred of the Church or denial of the doctrine of the resurrection of the body.

If cremation has been chosen, the Church prefers that the body be brought to the church for the funeral Mass and then taken to the crematorium. If it is physically or morally impossible for the body to be present, it is permitted to celebrate the funeral service without it.

Recommended Reading

Stravinskas, Rev. Peter M. J., *The Catholic Answer Book,* Our Sunday Visitor, Huntington, IN 46750, 1990, pp. 150-151.

Q. What do the letters I.N.R.I. above the cross stand for and what is the meaning?

A. John 19:19-20 KJV gives us the answer to this question:

> "And Pilate wrote a title, and put it on the cross. And the writing was, JESUS OF NAZARETH THE KING OF THE JEWS. This title then read many of the Jews: for the place where Jesus was crucified was nigh to the city: and it was written in Hebrew, and Greek, and Latin."

The letters I.N.R.I. represent the first letters of the Latin inscription "Jesus Nazarenus Rex ludaeorum."

Q. Why have the tabernacles been removed from the center of the altars in some cases to other rooms?

A. The Sacred Congregation for the Sacraments and Divine Worship document *Inaestimabile donum*, dated 3 April 1980, paragraph 24 says,

> "The tabernacle in which the Eucharist is kept can be located on an altar, or away from it, in a spot in the

> church which is very prominent, truly noble and duly decorated, or in a chapel suitable for private prayer and for adoration by the faithful."

This would allow placement of the tabernacle just about anywhere so long as it is suitably adorned and available for adoration by the faithful.

Section 2 of Canon 938 of the *1983 Code of Canon Law* says,

> "The tabernacle in which the blessed Eucharist is reserved should be sited in a distinguished place in the church or oratory, a place which is conspicuous, suitably adorned and conducive to prayer."

This later document of the church, with the addition of the word "conspicuous" would appear to rule out a separate chapel in most parish churches. Neither "prominent" nor "conspicuous" mean that the tabernacle should be located dead center in the sanctuary, but they could certainly imply that it should be visible from the central axis of the church.

<u>Recommended Reading:</u>

Drummey, James J., *Catholic Replies,* C. R. Publications, Norwood, MA 02062, 1995, pp. 253-254.

Stravinskas, Rev. Peter M. J., *The Catholic Answer Book 2,* Our Sunday Visitor, Huntington, IN 46750, 1994, pp. 186-187.

Q. During the Eucharistic Prayer, how do we know which mystery of faith to proclaim?

A. There are three choices for the memorial acclamation during the Eucharistic Prayer and the choice is left up to the priest or, if the priest so delegates, to the cantor or song leader. We know which choice has been made by the first word of the acclamation:

1. "We proclaim your death, O Lord …"
2. "When we eat this bread and drink this cup …"
3. "Save us, Savior of the world …"

Likewise, if the number of the Eucharistic Prayer is not announced, it can be found from the opening words:

Eucharistic Prayer I – "To you, therefore most merciful Father …"
Eucharistic Prayer II – "You are indeed Holy, O Lord, the fount of all holiness."
Eucharistic Prayer III – "You are indeed Holy, O Lord, and all You have created."
Eucharistic Prayer IV – "We give You praise, Father Most Holy."

Q. Why do you say written prayers? They are not as meaningful as prayers from the heart.

A. Who says a written prayer is not from the heart? God knows our most innermost thoughts and needs; whether we are praying a written prayer or ad-libbing it as we go. The sincerity of the prayer is shown not in the words said, but in the recognition of the need for and the response to the desire to pray. When asked by one of His disciples to teach them how to pray, Jesus didn't tell them to make something up from the heart on the spot, He said,

> "When you pray, say, Our Father, which art in heaven, Hallowed be thy name ..." (Luke 11:2-4 KJV).

Q. Why can Catholics go to church on Saturdays and we cannot?

A. The Jewish Sabbath is Saturday. As with Jewish tradition, the liturgical day begins the evening before. The Jewish tradition is that the day starts at sundown and this was carried over into Christian tradition by praying the First Vespers for the day on the evening before. After Vatican II, in recognition of the obligation that all Catholics have to attend Sunday Mass and the fact that some individuals were required to work on Sunday, an evening Mass of anticipation (or vigil Mass) was instituted. This vigil Mass usually starts before sundown, thereby fulfilling the commandment to "Keep the Sabbath day holy", although this is accidental.

Even though the original intent was to assist workers, those who had to travel, and vacationers, the sad fact is that the privilege has been abused and some now never attend Mass on Sunday. Part of our obligation to keep the Sabbath day holy is to attend Mass on Sunday whenever possible.

<u>Recommended Reading:</u>

Stravinskas, Rev. Peter M. J., *The Catholic Answer Book,* Our Sunday Visitor, Huntington, IN 46750, 1990, p. 117.

Q. Why does the Catholic Church believe that it is the only true Christian church?
Q. What about other churches?

A. Jesus said:

> "'Thou art Peter, and upon this rock I will build my church; and the gates of hell shall not prevail against it.'" (Matthew 16:18 KJV);

> "'Neither pray I for these alone, but for them also which shall believe on me through their word; That they all may be one; as thou, Father, art in me, and I in thee, that they also may be one in us: that the world may believe that thou hast sent me.' (John 17:20-23 KJV);

> "'Go ye therefore, and teach all nations, baptizing them in the name of the Father, and of the Son, and of the Holy Ghost: Teaching them to observe all things whatsoever I have commanded you: and, lo, I am with you always, even unto the end of the world.'" (Matthew 28:19-20 KJV).

Jesus established only one church, the one He founded on Peter, the rock. He prayed that all His followers would be one, and He promised that He would be with His Church until the end of the world. This was recognized by Saint Paul when he wrote:

> "Make every effort to keep the unity of the Spirit through the bond of peace. There is one body and one Spirit, just

> as you were called to one hope when you were called one Lord, one faith, one baptism; one God and Father of all, who is over all and through all and in all." (Ephesians 4:3-6 NIV).

One faith means one set of beliefs, one set of doctrines; doctrines which never change. There is only one Catholic Church but there are over 34 ,000 Protestant denominations today; each separated from the other by differing doctrines. Each of these denominations can be traced back to a single individual who was not Saint Peter or one of the Apostles.

Every Christian church possesses some of the truths revealed by Our Lord but only the Catholic Church can trace its origins all the way back to Jesus and Saint Peter through the Rite of Ordination, the laying on of hands and passing on of episcopal responsibility and authority. Since only the Catholic Church can be traced all the way back to Jesus, only the Catholic Church can be said to possess all the revealed truth. After all, Jesus founded the Church, promised that the gates of hell would not prevail against it (which means that it would be perpetual and not teach error) and promised to be with it until the end of time. Not at the end of time, but continually until the end of time. Either the Catholic Church was, and is, the one true Church, or the Bible is wrong, or Jesus lied.

Recommended Reading:

Hayes, Rev. Edward J., Hayes, Rev. Msgr. Paul J., & Drummey, James J., *Catholicism & Reason,* Prow Books, Libertyville, IL 60048, 1981, pp. 91-154.

Nevins, Albert J., *Answering A Fundamentalist,* Our Sunday Visitor, Huntington, IN 46750, 1990, pp. 31-40.

Schreck, Alan, *Your Catholic Faith,* Redeemer Books/Servant Publications, Ann Arbor, MI 48107, 1989, pp. 39-55.

Drummey, James J., *Catholic Replies,* C. R. Publications, Norwood, MA 02062, 1995, pp. 58-59, 90-94.

Rumble, Rev. Dr. Leslie & Carty, Rev. Charles Mortimer, *Radio Replies, Third Volume,* TAN Books & Publishers, Rockford, IL 61105, 1979, paras. 462-463.

Q. Why force non-Catholic spouses to raise children in the Catholic Church?

A. The Non-Catholic spouse is not forced to raise children in the Catholic faith. The non-Catholic party must be informed by the priest that the Catholic spouse must do everything in their power to see that any children born of the union are baptized and raised in the Catholic faith. The non-Catholic does not have to agree, but must acknowledge that they have been informed of the intention of the Catholic partner.

That said, let's look at the situation from the Catholic point of view. Most non-Catholics do not believe that their faith is the one true faith. Instead, they believe that one faith is as good, or almost as good, as another. As such, their conscience does not forbid that their children be brought up in the Catholic faith. The Catholic partner on the other hand, has sure knowledge that the Catholic Church is the one true Church, and therefore, one faith is not as good as another. By raising the children Catholic, the Catholic parent is following the admonition of Jesus that the Church be one.

Q. When and who said women no longer had to cover their head with a veil?

A. The 1917 Code of Canon Law contained a provision requiring women to wear a veil or hat to cover their heads in church. This was based on St. Paul's comments on the conduct of men and women at public worship services (1 Corinthians 11:2-16). The Sacred Congregation for the Doctrine of the Faith, in its declaration, *Inter Insigniores*, dated 15 October 1976, states that the obligation imposed upon women to wear a covering on the head was probably inspired by the customs of the period and as such, it constitutes a disciplinary practice of minor importance that no longer has a normative value.

The provision to wear a head covering does not appear in the *1983 Code of Canon Law.* This does not prevent a woman from wearing a head covering if she so desires, but she is no longer required to do so.

Q. During Mass you light different candles and put out others. Please explain.

A. Throughout the centuries, candles have been used for honorary reasons, such as carrying them ahead of the celebrant as a sign of respect and for religious purposes, giving symbolic emphasis to the candle, as a symbol of Christ. Candles at Mass became obligatory only in the 17th century. In an ordinary Mass, two lighted candles are required. In a more festive Mass, six are allowed with a seventh being added at Mass celebrated by a bishop.

Recommended Reading:

Lang, Rev. Jovian P., *Dictionary of the Liturgy,* Catholic Book Publishing Company, New York, NY, 1989, pp. 79-80.

Q. Please explain how the Church can change their rules? Not God's Law.

A. Within the Church there are two main types of law: Divine (God's) law and Church law. Divine law is those revealed truths which God has entrusted to His Church for safekeeping and instruction of the faithful. Examples of Divine law are the 10 Commandments and the Church dogmas (there is one God, there are 3 Persons in the One God, there are 2 natures in the One Person of God the Son, grace is a gift of God, Jesus founded the Church in order to continue His work of redemption for all time, abortion is murder, etc.). Divine law cannot be changed by the Church or anyone else as it is God's revealed truth.

Church law constitutes those earthly rules and regulations which the Church has found necessary to enact to ensure that the great commission given to the Church by Christ is fulfilled:

> "'Therefore go and make disciples of all nations, baptizing them in the name of the Father and of the Son and of the Holy Spirit, and teaching them to obey everything I have commanded you. And surely I am with you always, to the very end of the age.'" (Matthew 28:19-20 NIV).

As was explained in the chapter titled "THE PAPACY", the ability to make these rules was given to the Church by Jesus Himself and is referred to as "the ability to bind and loose". Church law covers a large variety of rules for the Universal Church (for example; the Code of Canon Law, of which there are 1752 canons) as well as rules unique to a particular region or diocese. Examples of Church law would be whether priests may marry, how long a fast is to be observed before receiving Holy Communion, and what training and instruction is required to be recognized as an extraordinary minister of the Eucharist. Church laws can be changed by the authority which enacted them.

Recommended Reading:

Catechism of the Catholic Church, Libreria Editrice Vaticana, 1994, paras. 1950-1986, 2030-2051.

Hayes, Rev. Edward J., Hayes, Rev. Msgr. Paul J., & Drummey, James J., *Catholicism & Reason,* Prow Books, Libertyville, IL 60048, 1981, pp. 127-136.

Rumble, Rev. Dr. Leslie & Carty, Rev. Charles Mortimer, *Radio Replies, First Volume,* TAN Books & Publishers, Rockford, IL 61105, 1979, paras. 224, 276, 331-335, 570, 596-614, 622-627, 793.

Rumble, Rev. Dr. Leslie & Carty, Rev. Charles Mortimer, *Radio Replies, Second Volume*, TAN Books & Publishers, Rockford, IL 61105, 1979, paras. 365, 472-473.

Rumble, Rev. Dr. Leslie & Carty, Rev. Charles Mortimer, *Radio Replies, Third Volume*, TAN Books & Publishers, Rockford, IL 61105, 1979, paras. 499, 1122.

Ott, Dr. Ludwig, *Fundamentals of Catholic Dogma*, TAN Books, Rockford, IL 61105, 1974.

Coriden, James A., *An Introduction to Canon Law*, Paulist Press, Mahwah, NJ 07430, 1991.

Q. Shouldn't all nuns wear habits?

A. In the *1983 Code of Canon Law*, Canon 669 reads:

> Section 1, "Religious are to wear the habit of their institute, made according to the norm of proper law, as a sign of their consecration and as a witness to poverty."
>
> Section 2, "Clerical religious of an institute which does not have a proper habit are to wear clerical dress according to the norm of can. 284."

Canon 284 says that Clerics are to wear suitable ecclesiastical garb according to the norms issued by the conference of bishops and according to legitimate local customs.

It should be noted that these requirements apply to all Religious; not only to nuns, but also to brothers and priests. It is unfortunate that some religious communities have chosen to mask their identity by adopting as their "uniform" a symbol which can be easily mistaken for a piece of costume jewelry. The ultimate authority for enforcing these requirements of Canon Law falls upon the bishops who are responsible for all Religious working in their dioceses.

<u>Recommended Reading:</u>

Stravinskas, Rev. Peter M. J., *The Catholic Answer Book,* Our Sunday Visitor, Huntington, IN 46750, 1990, pp. 173-174.

Q. Explain the parts of the Mass.

A. This is a tall order. What we will attempt to do here, in the limited space available for such an endeavor, is to very briefly describe the significance of the various parts of the Mass. For a more detailed background and explanation, the inquirer can attend the Rite of Christian Initiation of Adults (R.C.I.A.) classes in their parish.

Entry Procession: Preceded by the crucifix, which reminds us of why we are at the Mass, the *Book of the Gospels* is brought into the assembly of the faithful followed by the priest who will preside at the Holy Sacrifice.

Penitential Rite: Led by the priest, all the faithful profess to God and our fellow man our sorrow and repentance for the sins we have committed. These sins are sins of thought, speech, action, and inaction.

Gloria: (omitted during Lent and Advent). This song of joy proclaims the glory of God and what He has done for us through Jesus the Christ.

Opening Prayer: The priest sets the theme for the Mass of the day.

First Reading: The first reading, usually taken from the Old Testament, has been chosen because of its association with the Gospel reading which follows. As we listen to God's Word being proclaimed, we may realize how little humanity's response to God's call has changed over the centuries.

Responsorial Psalm: This psalm is chosen because of its reflection of one of the themes of the first reading. As we listen and respond, we gain a deeper understanding of the first reading and of God's plan for us all.

Second Reading: Chosen from one of the epistles, this reading is not necessarily connected to the first reading or to the Gospel reading. The second readings work their way chronologically through one epistle at a time. As we listen to the second reading every week, we relate it back to the second reading of the previous weeks so we can better understand the message of the epistle being proclaimed.

Gospel: Like the second reading, the Gospel readings progress in chronological order (except that the seasons of Advent or Lent emphasize the events leading up to the Birth or Passion of Our Lord, respectively). As we hear the Gospel being proclaimed, we realize how Jesus has indeed fulfilled the promises of the Old Testament and enabled us to approach God and have our sins forgiven.

Homily: We listen as the priest or deacon explains how one or more of the readings for this day have application to our life.

Profession of Faith: If anyone were to ask us what we believe as a Catholic, all we would need to do is recite this profession of faith to them. This profession is what is called the Nicene Creed and was formulated for the most part by the Council of Nicaea (325 A.D.) and the Council of Constantinople (381 A.D.).

General Intercession: We join in offering the prayers and needs of the community to God.

Collection: A monetary collection is taken up at this point. We know that whatever money we contribute to the collection will be used by the Church to further God's work.

Preparation of the Gifts: Gifts of bread and wine have been brought to the altar as an offering from the community to God. These gifts return to Him that which He has created and are freely offered out of gratitude for His generosity.

Eucharistic Prayer: As we say this prayer to God, we place our own life on the altar ("Lift up your hearts. We lift them up to the Lord") along with the other gifts of the community. We recognize that our very being is a gift from God which we freely offer back to Him.

Holy, Holy, Holy: By joining in this acclamation, we join in the prayer of the angels (Isaiah 6:3) and the praise of the crowds on that first Palm Sunday (Mark 11:9-10).

Eucharistic Prayer I. II. III. or IV: As the priest recites this prayer, we listen as he fulfills the commandment given to the Apostles at the Last Supper: "Do this in memory of me." By reciting the words of consecration, the priest, empowered by Christ Himself, makes Jesus present Body, Blood, Soul and Divinity under the appearances of bread and wine for the nourishment of our soul. We are joined with Jesus and the Apostles at the Last Supper as the event is made present for us.

Lord's Prayer: As individuals and as members of the community of the faithful, we pray the prayer which Jesus Himself taught His followers.

Breaking of the Bread: The gifts which have been brought to the altar and transformed by God into His gift to us are readied for distribution to the faithful.

Communion: Provided we are free from mortal sin, we go forward to receive God's gift to us, which is the Body and Blood of Our Lord, Jesus Christ. This is the gift which was promised by Jesus in John 6:25-69 and is not nourishment for our body, but for our soul.

Prayer After Communion: We give thanks to God the Father for the many blessings and gifts He has given to us. We especially give thanks for the gift of His Son in the Eucharist.

Concluding Rite: We receive God's blessing through the priest and are dismissed to go among the community, empowered by Jesus' own Body and Blood, and to live out the Gospel message

Recessional: Preceded by the crucifix, which reminds us why we were at the Offering of the Holy Sacrifice of the Mass, the faithful process out.

SACRAMENTALS

Q. Why does the Church use sacramentals?

A. A sacramental is a sacred sign by which spiritual effects especially are signified and are obtained by the intercession of the Church (Canon 1166). These sacred signs bear a resemblance to the sacraments (discussed in a later chapter) in that they signify effects, particularly of a spiritual kind. Sacramentals take various forms from blessings to blessed objects. Sacramentals with which we are all familiar are making the sign of the cross (blessing ourselves), holy water (water which has been blessed by a priest or deacon), etc.

Sacramentals, as a rule, were not instituted by Christ (exorcism would be an obvious exception), but by the Church. As such, sacramentals do not confer the grace of the Holy Spirit in the way that the sacraments do, but by the Church's intercessory prayer they do prepare us to receive God's grace and dispose us to cooperate with it. The efficacy of sacramental depends upon the devotion, faith and love of those who use them. Sacramentals serve to remind the faithful of the Glory of God and thereby to draw us closer to Him. The prayer over a meal (blessing the meal) for example, reminds us that all that we have comes from God's love for us and this reminder helps us to be open to receiving even more of God's bounty.

Recommended Reading:

Catechism of the Catholic Church, Libreria Editrice Vaticana, 1994, paras. 1667-1679.

Ott, Dr. Ludwig, *Fundamentals of Catholic Dogma,* TAN Books and Publishers, Rockford, IL 61105, 1974, pp. 348-349.

Q. Why do Catholics make the sign of the cross?

Q. Why do we make the sign of the cross with and without holy water?

A. The sign of the cross and holy water are both sacramentals as discussed in the preceding question. In making the sign of the cross we, as Christians, are performing a sacramental act which dates back to at least the second century where it was used as a sign of recognition among Christians as well as a blessing.

In making the sign of the cross, we affirm our belief in two of the basic mysteries of our faith:

1. The words, "In the name of the Father, and of the Son, and of the Holy Spirit", affirm our belief in a Triune God - Three Persons in One God.
2. By tracing the shape of the cross on our body we affirm our belief that by His death on the cross, Jesus achieved our redemption. Finally, Jesus tells us that the greatest commandment is:

> "Love the Lord your God with all your heart and with all your soul and with all your mind and with all your strength." (Mark 12:30 NIV).

By the various parts of our body which we touch as we trace out the sign of the cross, we affirm this teaching: mind (forehead), heart and soul (chest), and strength (shoulders). This is not a new commandment instituted by Jesus, but is in fact a part of the *Shema* (Deuteronomy 6:5) which was (and is) prayed daily by every devout Jew. When making the sign of the cross after dipping our fingers into the holy water, we are blessing ourselves with holy water and renewing our baptismal promises (vows).

<u>Recommended Reading:</u>

Fernandez, Erasto, "All About the Sign of the Cross", *Catholic Digest*, August 1994.

Dodd, Bill, "Test Your Strength in Sacramentals", *Catholic Digest*, December 1994.

Q. Medals and crosses are not understood by other religions. Why do Catholics wear medals and crosses?

A. Medals and crosses which have been blessed are sacramentals. If they have not been blessed, they are simply considered jewelry. The use in the Church of medals is very ancient and is intended to excite devotion and prayer. These items also signify the individual Christian's commitment to a holy life or commendation to the particular protection of the subject depicted.

Just like with all sacramentals, there is no "magic" benefit derived from wearing a medal, but they do prepare the wearer to receive God's grace and dispose them to cooperate with it. The efficacy of a sacramental depends upon the devotion, faith and love of the person who uses it.

Q. What is a scapular?

Q. Why do Catholics wear a scapular?

Q. What is the proper way to wear a scapular?

A. In the beginning, a scapular was a sort of work apron which came to symbolize the cross or yoke of Christ. They were originally shoulder-wide strips of cloth worn over the tunic and reaching almost to the ground in front and in back. By the 11th century, scapulars had become part of the habit of religious orders. Now, they are two small squares of cloth joined by strings and worn about the neck by lay persons. Scapulars are worn as a sign of association with a religious order and for devotional purposes.

There are certain promises attached to wearing a scapular and living at the same time as a faithful follower of Christ. Among these is that the Blessed Virgin will intercede for the wearer at the time of their death. The mere wearing of a couple of pieces of cloth is no guarantee to heaven, however, to believe this would be to engage in superstition. Like all sacramentals, the scapular does remind the wearer of the exemplary life they are to live and of the rewards which await them if they do live that life.

There have been nearly 20 different scapulars recognized by the Catholic Church, all of them are worn around the neck, either over or under other clothing. Scapulars associated with religious orders do also require the lay wearer to be dedicated to that particular order.

Recommended Reading:

Drummey, James J., *Catholic Replies,* C. R. Publications, Norwood, MA 02062, 1995, p. 130.

Meagher, Paul K. OP, O'Brien, Thomas C. & Aherne, Sister Consuelo M. SSJ, *Encyclopedic Dictionary of Religion,* Corpus Publications, Washington, D.C., 1979, p. 3208.

Q. What are the uses of holy water?

A. Holy water is used for baptism and rites of blessing and purification. Originally, holy water blessed at the Easter Vigil was kept throughout the entire year for these purposes. Now, with the appearance of large parishes, the logistics of storing this water for later use is almost insurmountable. Currently, blessed "Easter water" is used in the parish during the Easter season. After the season is ended, water is blessed every time the need arises.

Recommended Reading:

Stravinskas, Rev. Peter M. J., *Our Sunday Visitor's Catholic Encyclopedia,* Our Sunday Visitor, Huntington, IN 46750, 1991, p. 482.

Q. What are "blessed" objects?

A. A blessed object is any object over which an ordained clergyman (priest or deacon) has pronounced a blessing. The act of blessing sanctifies the object for use in prayer and devotion. The concept of blessing is prevalent in the Old Testament where it is conceived as a communication of life from God. As such, the firstborn of the family received the blessing of the father (remember Jacob and Esau?). With the blessing came vigor, strength, and success. The sacred vessels and the tabernacle were consecrated to God. Consecration means to set aside something for religious purposes.

Sometimes the truth of an action comes from a most unlikely source. A priest said that a small child came to him to have an object blessed. When the priest asked him if he knew what it meant when something was blessed, the child replied, "It means it has been touched by God." Try reading the Beatitudes (Matthew 5:1-12) and everywhere you read "Blessed" substitute "Touched by God." It will give you a much deeper understanding of the meaning of blessing and having an object blessed.

In 1984, a *Book of Blessings* was published. This contains blessings for persons, objects, and events.

Q. What is blessed salt?

A. Matthew 5:13 compares salt to the integrity of one's life and Colossians 4:6 makes a similar comparison between salt and Christian wisdom. For these reasons as well as the fact that salt is seen as a sign of purity and preservation, salt was customarily used during the baptismal rite of infants, where it was placed on the lips. Following the example of purification through the use of salt by the Prophet Elisha in 2 Kings 2:21, salt was also used in the blessing of holy water and in the rite of the consecration of a church building and an altar.

In the present form of the liturgy, blessed salt may be mixed with newly blessed holy water.

Recommended Reading:

Stravinskas, Rev. Peter M. J., *Our Sunday Visitors Catholic Encyclopedia,* Our Sunday Visitor, Huntington, IN 46750, 1991, p. 861.

HISTORY

Q. How do you know that Jesus started the Catholic faith?
Q. How can you know that the Catholic Church is the one that Jesus founded?

A. Because Jesus told Simon at the same time that He changed his name to Peter:

> "And I tell you that you are Peter [means rock], and on this rock I will build my church, and the gates of Hades [or hell] will not overcome it." (Matthew 16:18 NIV, brackets from footnotes).

No denomination other than Catholic can trace their roots in an unbroken succession all the way back to Peter and the Apostles. A succession that has been manifested by the laying on of hands. Every other Christian denomination can ultimately trace their roots back to some individual and time when they separated from the Church built on Peter and the faith which that Church teaches.

In His great commission, Jesus told the eleven Apostles (Judas had hung himself and Matthias had not yet been chosen to replace him):

> "'All authority in heaven and on earth has been given to me. Therefore go and make disciples of all nations, baptizing them in the name of the Father and of the Son and of the Holy Spirit, and teaching them to obey everything I have commanded you. And surely I am with you always, to the very end of the age.'" (Matthew 28:18-20 NIV).

These eleven Apostles were the first Bishops of the Church, with Peter as their leader (see the chapter titled "THE PAPACY"). Notice that Jesus promised to be with this Church and its leaders "always, to the very end of the age" and that "the gates of Hades will not overcome it". This means that the Church will be divinely protected in its teaching until the end of time. Unless the Bible is wrong or Jesus lied, that Church is the Catholic Church. This also precludes the possibility of the Church going into error at some time in history. Some of the things the Church teaches may not be what we want to hear, but the command is to teach everything, not just the nice, easy-to-obey things.

Recommended Reading:

"Peter and the Papacy", A Catholic Answers Tract, Catholic Answers, P.O. Box 17490, San Diego, CA 92177.

Q. Since there is antiquity in the Greek and Slavic churches, how can the Roman Church claim to be the real Church of Christ?

A. Granted, there is antiquity in the Greek and other Orthodox churches. I will refer to all these churches as Eastern Orthodox Churches. They too can trace their origins back to Christ and the

Apostles. The Catholic Church can (and does) claim to be the Church which was founded by Jesus because it is founded on Peter, the first Pope; as noted in the answer to the preceding question. The Eastern Orthodox Churches do not claim that the Catholic Church left them; they admit that they split away from the Catholic Church (and the Pope) in what is now generally referred to as having happened in 1054 A.D. In fact, there was no one date which can be pointed to as being the exact moment of division. Points of contention between the Orthodox and Catholic groups focused upon:

1. The Catholic Church's decision to teach that the Holy Spirit comes from the Father and the Son ("filoque") and is expressed in the Creed,
2. The issue of clerical celibacy, and
3. The Catholic contention that the Pope is the ultimate determiner of doctrine and discipline in the Church.

Recommended Reading:

Meagher, Paul K. OP, O'Brien, Thomas C. & Aherne, Sister Consuelo M. SSJ, *Encyclopedic Dictionary of Religion,* Corpus Publications, Washington, D.C., 1979, pp. 1143-1144.

Q. How can the Catholic Church be the "true" church when some priests do evil things?

A. You are confusing the infallibility of the Church with incapability of its leaders and members to commit sin. The Catholic Church is not a home for Saints, it is a hospital for sinners. Every individual is a sinner, even the Pope goes to confession once a week.

The doctrines the Church teaches are the true teachings of Jesus. How the priests, the bishops and the leaders conduct themselves is an entirely different matter. Anyone who causes scandal brings shame upon himself and the organization he represents.

Before Jesus established His Church, He recognized that teaching authority resided in the leaders of the Jewish community, and that they were causing scandal:

> "The teachers of the law and the Pharisees sit in Moses' seat. So you must be careful to do everything they tell you. But do not do what they do, for they do not practice what they preach." (Matthew 23:2-3 NIV).

Jesus also anticipated that even this problem would exist in His Church. He chose 12 Apostles. He chose one whom He knew was going to betray Him. This is where we get the expression "Judas priest". As we look at the leadership of the Church over its almost 2,000 year history, at no time has the number of Judas priests come anywhere near as high as that original 8.3 percent (1 out of 12).

When one hears of a priest causing scandal, the immediate thought is of pedophile priests because of the recent publicity which has been given to this problem. In the interest of fairness, it should be pointed out that the incidence of pedophilia in the married Protestant clergy is greater than the level among Catholic priests. This does not excuse any priest who betrays his trust, but hopefully it will help to put the problem into a more balanced perspective.

Q. What is the Inquisition?

A. There were at least three: The Papal Inquisition, The Spanish Inquisition, and The Roman Inquisition.

1. **The Papal Inquisition** was an outgrowth of the Council of Toulouse held in 1229 (not an ecumenical council) where a special ecclesiastical tribunal was established to counter the heresy of Albigensianism, which taught that all matter, including the body, was created by evil while the spirit was created by good. Until 1231, the duty of detecting and repressing heresy had fallen on the bishop, but in 1231, Pope Gregory IX appointed a number of Papal Inquisitors. Pope Gregory IX was opposed to torture, but Pope Innocent IV approved its use for the discovery of heresy, and Pope Urban IV confirmed this usage, which like the death penalty for heresy, had its origins in the Roman Law. Although intended for all Christendom, it was active primarily in southern France. This Inquisition died out around 1300 with the demise of Albigensianism.
2. **The Spanish Inquisition** was a state rather than church inquisition. Established in 1481 by King Ferdinand and Queen Isabella, the king appointed the Grand Inquisitor and the other officials, and also signed the decrees; the penalties were inflicted in his name. The purpose of this Inquisition was to remove any potential traitors (secret Muslims or Jews) who might aid in any Muslim attack or any internal uprising. At that point in history, Spain was the only country which had allowed Muslims and Jews to remain within their boundaries.

The Inquisition was triggered by a Turkish storming of the Italian city of Otranto in 1480. The Turks put some 12,000 people (half the population of the city) to death, including every priest in the city, and sawed the Archbishop in two. They offered to spare many of their captive's lives if they would embrace the Muslim faith. Pope Sixtus IV approved the Spanish Inquisition because he was under the impression that an ecclesiastical inquisition was to be established, but when the true state of the case was brought to his knowledge the following year, it was too late. All that he and his successors could do was to protest against its excesses, which they did. The Spanish Inquisition was abolished in 1834. There were no council actions (ecumenical or otherwise) involved in this Inquisition and the papal approval, brief that it was, was not and did not claim to be an infallible action. The Spanish Inquisition is addressed fairly accurately in almost any encyclopedia although many secular discussions are distorted to widely varying degrees, particularly in the area of the number of "casualties". This is the Inquisition most anti-Catholics emphasis when they attempt to discredit the Church. Complete records of the Spanish Inquisition do not exist, but it is recorded that between 1540 and 1700 a total of 100,000 cases were tried with 10,000 individuals being submitted to torture and 828 individuals being put to death. It should also not be forgotten that John Calvin, the founder of the "Reformed" churches, burned Michael Servetus at the stake for heresy and established his own inquisition in Geneva for the punishment of unmanageable Christians.

3. **The Roman Inquisition** began in 1542 and was the least active and most benign of the three Inquisitions. This is the Inquisition which tried Galileo. The Galileo affair was a matter of science, not religion. It did indirectly concern the Church and spiritual interests because of the circumstances of the time, and Galileo's own diversion into theological speculations. Galileo would not have clashed with religion had he not interjected his own interpretations of Sacred Scripture regarding what he thought to be a contradiction between the Bible and the scientific discoveries. The Catholic Church, as Church, did not digress from spiritual matters in the Galileo case. Some people, at the time, ridiculed Scripture regarding the sun, etc. Because of the spiritual implications, the Church was seriously concerned. There were unfortunate decisions made in connection with the Galileo case, but it was not a decision involving the infallibility of the Church. Church infallibility involves only matters of faith and morals, not natural science, geography, trigonometry, etc.

Of these Inquisitions, only the first and the last had any lasting support of the Church. The important thing to remember about the Spanish Inquisition is that, although the methods which were used are repugnant to today's society, they employed means which were in common use at the time and their operation must be understood within the framework of the period in which they operated. In the Middle Ages, a man convicted of even a small theft was frequently punished by death, and the penalty for murder by poison was death by unspeakable torture. In the sixteenth century, a man convicted of high treason was tortured for hours and then disemboweled alive. At the time of the American Revolution, a mutineer was either flogged to death or hanged from the yardarm, the outer portions of the yard of the square sail. It was only in the last hundred years that police in the United States were forced to give up the "third degree" or intensive questioning and rough treatment in order to get a confession from a suspect.

Recommended Reading:

Catechism of the Catholic Church, Libreria Editrice Vaticana, 1994, para. 2298.

"The Inquisition", A Catholic Answers Tract, Catholic Answers, P.O. Box 17490, San Diego, CA 92177.

Minis, Jeffrey A., Carroll, Warren H., Marshner, William H, & Burns, Kristin M. P., *Reasons for Hope,* Christendom College Press, Front Royal, VA 22630, pp. 197-205, 213-218.

Q. If Catholic doctrine has never changed, why were some doctrines supported by Councils or Papal Decrees in later centuries? (If the Church teaches that a doctrine is true because a certain council in a certain year says so, does this mean the doctrine was "new" in the year of the council?)

A. Doctrine means "what is taught". Dogma, in Catholic theology, is a truth that the Church requires the faithful to accept as a doctrine revealed by God. When a council or Papal decree pronounces a matter of doctrine, this does not mean that the doctrine was "new" at the time of pronouncement. In fact, doctrine develops over time as understanding of the subject grows and becomes clearer. Most Councils were convened to answer a question (or heresy). The pronouncement of the Council states the teaching of the Church on the matter: for example, The First Council of Nicaea (325) answered Arianism; The Council of Ephesus (431) answered Nestorianism; and The Council of Trent (1545-1563) answered the Protestant Reformation.

Recommended Reading:

Meagher, Paul K. OP, O'Brien, Thomas C. & Aherne, Sister Consuelo M. SSJ, *Encyclopedic Dictionary of Religion,* Corpus Publications, Washington, D.C., 1979, pp. 1083-1085.

"Can Dogma Develop?", A Catholic Answers Tract, Catholic Answers, P.O. Box 17490, San Diego, CA 92177.

SALVATION/JUSTIFICATION

Q. Have you been saved? Is this the same as having been baptized and confirmed?
Q. We are often asked "Are you saved?"
Q. Being saved. Some people believe that once they accept Christ they are saved.

A. Salvation is not the same as baptism and confirmation. Baptism and confirmation will be discussed further in the chapter titled "SACRAMENTS". To properly answer questions concerning salvation, we must first define the terms. We Catholics and our separated brethren have different definitions for the words we commonly use.

Salvation: Catholics use this term to refer to the whole process, from its beginning in faith, through the whole Christian life of works in love on earth, to its completion in heaven. To our separated brethren this term means the initial step, like climbing aboard the ark of salvation, not the entire journey to the final destination. As you can see, the Catholic has a much broader meaning for the term "salvation" or "saved" while our non-Catholic brethren have a much narrower view.

Faith: To the Catholic, this is one of the three theological virtues [faith, hope and charity (love)]; faith is intellectual belief. To our separated brethren it is accepting Jesus with your whole heart and soul. In this case it is the Catholic who has the much narrower view while our non-Catholic brethren use it in a much broader sense.

With these definitions in mind, if someone asks you, "Have you been saved?", you can answer, "Yes, by the grace of God." This will answer the question from the point of view of the non-Catholic who asked it. A more correct answer, from the Catholic perspective would be:

1. I was saved at 3 o'clock on Good Friday when Jesus died on the Cross.
2. I am being saved by working out my salvation in fear and trembling (as St. Paul says in Philippians 2:12).
3. I will be saved by the grace of God.

Recommended Reading:

Catechism of the Catholic Church, Libreria Editrice Vaticana, 1994, paras. 161, 169.

Currie, David B., *Born Fundamentalist, Born Again Catholic,* Ignatius Press, San Francisco, CA 94122, 1996, pp. 109-141.

Kreeft, Peter & Tacelli, Ronald K., *Handbook of Christian Apologetics,* InterVarsity Press, Downers Grove, IL 60515, 1994, pp. 320-321.

"Assurance of Salvation", A Catholic Answers Tract, Catholic Answers, P.O. Box 17490, San Diego, CA 92177.

Q. Are Catholics taught that they are the only ones who will go to heaven?

A. No. The Catholic Church does teach that outside the Catholic Church there is no salvation, but one must look at what this really means. Paragraph 3 of the Second Vatican Council's Decree on Ecumenism (*Unitatis Redintegratio*, 21 November 1964) says that our separated brethren who believe in the faith of Christ and have been properly baptized are put in some, though imperfect, communion with the Catholic Church. It also says that those who have been justified by faith in baptism are incorporated into Christ, they therefore have a right to be called Christians, and with good reason are accepted as brothers by the children of the Catholic Church. Everyone is saved through the Catholic Church, either as faithful members of that Church, or as members of churches which contain some significant elements of truth and sanctification found in the Catholic Church, or as persons who, through no fault of their own, do not know the Gospel of Christ or His Church, but who nevertheless seek God with a sincere heart and, moved by grace, try in their actions to do His Will as they know it through the dictates of their conscience. For this reason, a bishop is responsible for every soul within his diocese, not just the Catholic ones.

<u>Recommended Reading:</u>

Catechism of the Catholic Church, Libreria Editrice Vaticana, 1994, paras. 846-847, 1271.

Drummey, James J., *Catholic Replies,* C. R. Publications, Norwood, MA 02062, 1995, pp. 90-100.

Q. Do Catholics believe you have to "work" your way into heaven (James 2:24)?
Q. Aren't we saved by faith alone?

A. One of the two basic tenets of the Protestant Reformation (Revolt) was sola fide (faith alone), the other being *sola scriptura* (only Scripture). *Sola scriptura* was addressed in the chapter titled "THE BIBLE".

What has been called "works righteousness" (earning a place in heaven) has been condemned as heresy by the Church. One cannot "work" their way into heaven, but neither is one saved by faith alone. One is saved by faith living in love. James 2:24 KJV says:

> "Ye see then how that by works a man is justified, and not by faith only."

What this means is that like Abram (Abraham), one must live out the faith they have in God. In Genesis 15:6 KJV we are told that Abram:

> "...believed in the Lord; and he credited it to him for righteousness."

But this is not when Abram's faith first manifests itself: Abram has been doing whatever God has asked of him since Genesis 12:1 (some 10 years earlier). In Luke 8:16 NIV, Jesus tells us in a parable about faith:

> "'No one lights a lamp and hides it in a clay jar or puts it under a bed. Instead, they put it on a stand, so that those who come in can see the light.'"

Likewise, we are to live out our faith so that it shines forth and enables others to come to the light of truth. Also, in the parable of the talents or bag of gold (Matthew 25:14-30), we are told of the fate of one who fails to put God's gifts to work; he is cast out. No one "earns" their way into heaven; to do so would be to put God under an obligation to bestow a gift that is His to give as He sees fit. The "works" which one does in living out their faith are works of love, not obligation. It says in Matthew 7:21 NIV,

> "Not everyone who says to me, 'Lord, Lord,' will enter the kingdom of heaven, but only the one who does the will of my Father who is in heaven."

And Ephesians 2:10 KJV,

> "For we are his workmanship, created in Christ Jesus unto good works, which God hath before ordained that we should walk in them."

Recommended Reading:

Hahn, Scott & Suprenant, Leon J. (Editors), *Catholic for a Reason,* Emmaus Road Press, 1998, pp. 87-105.

Q. Why is the Baptist belief that "Once saved, you're always saved" a heresy?

A. This belief isn't unique only to Baptists, many evangelicals and "nondenominational" groups also harbor this belief. The belief is not heretical, but it is mistaken and if taken to the extreme, could result in a sin against the Holy Spirit. It takes God for granted and presumes God's mercy and forgiveness.

Referring back to the definitions in the first question in this chapter, the non-Catholic believes that they are saved when they climb aboard the ark of salvation. Unfortunately, people fall off boats all the time. Some climb back on, and others drown. Our secular world is full of temptations which can lure us off the boat and into the sea of sin. Since nothing impure can enter heaven (Revelation 21:27), those who have not fully repented of their sins and gained God's forgiveness will not be able to disembark when the ark reaches its final destination (even though they may have swum alongside the whole way). One never has absolute assurance of their salvation until they arrive at the pearly gates and hear the message, "Well-done good and faithful servant", instead of, "Away from me you evildoer".

Recommended Reading:

"The Case of the Sinning Minister", A Catholic Answers Tract, Catholic Answers, P.O. Box 17490, San Diego, CA 92177.

Q. Please explain justification.

A. Justification is the process by which a person is made righteous, holy and pure before God. This is accomplished by the grace of the Holy Spirit working within us; empowering us to recognize and repent for our sins and avoid sins in the future. The grace working within us causes an interior conversion to take place so that we no longer desire things which we now recognize as sinful. In the Catholic tradition, our justification comes about through our faith in Christ and in a life of good works which are a response to God's invitation to believe.

St. Paul condemns claims that salvation comes through the "works of the law" (Romans 3:20 and Galatians 2:16; 3:10) but "works of the law" are different from the life of good works described above. Those who depended upon the "works of the law" were the Jews (like the Pharisees for example) who depended upon performing all the rituals prescribed in the *Book of the Law.* Such rituals were circumcision, ritual washing, temple sacrifices, avoiding certain foods, etc. (they had enumerated 613 laws which, if observed perfectly, made the individual righteous). The life of good works which the Catholic Christian lives is the life one lives because of their love for God and their fellow man. It is the life through which their faith enables them to radiate their hope and love. God has given unique gifts and abilities to every person; how we use these talents in our everyday lives are the good works upon which we will be judged (John 5:28-29).

Recommended Reading:

Catechism of the Catholic Church, Libreria Editrice Vaticana, 1994, paras. 1987-1995.

CHARISMATIC MOVEMENT

Q. Why is the Charismatic Movement coming into the Church?

A. The word "charismatic" derives from the Greek charisma which refers to the free gifts given to us by the Holy Spirit. Those involved in the Charismatic Movement share a personal experience which they call the "baptism of the Holy Spirit," through which God's Spirit renews them and fills them with grace. Some receive special gifts such as that of healing or speaking in tongues.

The Charismatic Movement in the Catholic Church has grown from a prayer group of some 20 individuals, faculty and students at Duquesne University, in Pittsburgh, Pennsylvania in 1966. It spread quickly to the University of Notre Dame, the Catholic students at the Michigan State University, the University of Iowa, University of Portland (Oregon), and elsewhere. At the present time, there are charismatic groups in most Catholic parishes in the United States.

The Catechism of the Catholic Church tells us that charismatic gifts are given to build up and strengthen the common good of the Church. As to why the Charismatic Movement is coming into the Catholic Church at the present time, only God knows for certain. It has been speculated that God has allowed the gifts of the Holy Spirit to be awakened in the Church, to shine forth as they did in the early centuries of the Church, in order to awaken the Church so that it will minister to all the souls who are being lured away to other denominations.

Recommended Reading:

Catechism of the Catholic Church, Libreria Editrice Vaticana, 1994, paras. 951, 2003.

O'Connor, Edward D., C.S.C., *The Pentecostal Movement in the Catholic Church,* Ave Maria Press, Notre Dame, IN 46556, 1971.

THE SACRAMENTS

Q. What is a sacrament?

A. The Baltimore Catechism tells us that a sacrament is an outward sign, instituted by Christ, to give grace. What this means, simply put, is that Jesus loves us so much that He still uses physical signs to communicate His love to us. We call these signs of love the Sacraments. Jesus' love is so great that the sacraments bring about what they symbolize. For example, in Baptism we are washed with water which symbolizes the soul being cleansed of sin. While the water is being poured over us, God makes that interior cleansing happen.

The Gospels all tell us that when Jesus walked this earth, He used physical signs to communicate his love. He touched the leper to cleanse him (Matthew 8:1-3); He gave bread and fish to the 5,000 (Luke 9:12-17); He healed the blind man with mud (John 9:6-7); and He took children in His arms and blessed them (Mark 10:13-16).

Jesus gave the Church seven Sacraments: Baptism, Confirmation and Eucharist are called the Sacraments of Initiation; Penance and Anointing of The Sick are called the Sacraments of Healing; and Matrimony and Holy Orders are called the Sacraments at the service of the community.

<u>Recommended Reading:</u>

Catechism of the Catholic Church, Libreria Editrice Vaticana, 1994, paras. 774, 947, 1113-1134.

Hardon, John A., S,J,, *The Catholic Catechism,* Doubleday, New York, NY 12020, 1981, pp. 457-547.

BAPTISM

Q. Why do you baptize infants?

A. Because we want salvation for our children, and 1 Peter 3:21 tells us that baptism saves us. Baptism washes away the stain of Original Sin, making the individual pure in the eyes of God, and places an indelible mark on the soul. This mark indicates that we belong to the Body of Christ. Colossians 2:11-12 tells us that baptism has replaced circumcision as the rite of initiation into God's family. Circumcision in the Old Testament was performed as a sign of the covenant between man and God at the age of 8 days:

> For the generations to come every male among you who is eight days old must be circumcised, including those in your household or bought with money from a foreigner – those who are not your offspring (Genesis 17:12 NIV).

Does God love infants and desire their salvation any less today than He did at the time of Abraham?

A conscious interaction does not have to take place between both parties in order for a personal relationship to exist. If it did, we would not have a personal relationship with our earthly family until several years after we were born. Babies, because they are God's children, have a very personal relationship with God. They may not have any concept of who God is, but this doesn't prevent God from caring for the child, protecting it, and sending His blessings upon it.

Infant baptism has been practiced since very early in the history of the Church. There are writings from the 2nd century which attest to this practice, and the Bible itself refers to whole households which received baptism; no doubt including the infants therein (Acts 16:15; 18:8, 1 Corinthians 1:16). There is nothing in Holy Scripture which erects barriers to, or forbids, infant baptism.

Recommended Reading:

Catechism of the Catholic Church, Libreria Editrice Vaticana, 1994, paras. 1213-1284 (especially 1250-1252).

"Personal Relationship?", *This Rock*, The Magazine of Catholic Apologetics & Evangelization, October 1996, p. 41.

Q. Where do babies that die before they are baptized go?

A. Just exactly where unbaptized babies go when they die is uncertain. Holy Scripture is silent on this point but we do know that no soul will ever be lost except through their own fault.

The ordinary means of salvation is by Baptism, but God can supply the grace usually given by baptism in a way which has not been revealed to us. We believe that children who aren't baptized are entrusted to the mysterious but infinitely kind and powerful love of God who wants all His creation to be with Him in heaven.

Q. What's the difference between John the Baptist's baptism and a Christian baptism (Acts 19:4-5)?

A. John's baptism was a baptism of repentance (Mark 1:4-5). It was a baptism of water only. Participation in John's baptism expressed a person's willingness to change and God's willingness to forgive sins before the coming of God's kingdom. The baptism of John did not remit sins, infuse God's grace, or incorporate the recipient into the Church.

On the other hand, a sacramental (Christian) baptism remits all previous sins, including the stain of Original Sin, infuses grace, and incorporates the recipient into the Church as a child of God, member of God's family, and part of the Body of Christ. It is a baptism of water and the Spirit (Matthew 3:11, John 3:5).

<u>Recommended Reading:</u>

Catechism of the Catholic Church, Libreria Editrice Vaticana, 1994, para. 720.

Hahn, Scott & Suprenant, Leon J. (Editors), *Catholic for a Reason,* Emmaus Road Press, 1998.

Q. Why do Catholics only pour water on the baptized instead of submerging them?

Q. Total submersion at baptism?

A. Nowhere in Holy Scripture does it tell us the mechanics of how to baptize an individual. The oldest writing that we have which describes the mechanics of baptism is in the *Didache* (also known as *The Teaching of the Lord to the Gentiles, Through the Twelve Apostles* or *The Teaching of the Twelve Apostles*) which has been dated by some scholars as early as 60 A.D. This places it before some of the New Testament was written. *Didache* 7:1-3 says: "Baptize as follows: after first explaining all these points, baptize in the name of the Father and of the Son and of the Holy Spirit, in running water. But if you have no running water, baptize in other water, and if you cannot in cold, then in warm. But if you have neither, pour water on the head three times in the name of the Father and of the Son and of the Holy Spirit."

The walls of the catacombs contain drawings of candidates standing ankle-deep in water while the water of baptism is poured over their head.

The Code of Canon Law allows Baptism by immersion, by pouring, or by sprinkling; depending upon the conditions involved and reflecting the earliest Christian practice.

<u>Recommended Reading:</u>

Catechism of the Catholic Church, Libreria Editrice Vaticana, 1994, paras. 1239-1240.

This Rock, The Magazine of Catholic Apologetics & Evangelization, September 1996, p. 43.

CONFIRMATION

Q. When you get confirmed at a particular time on a particular schedule, how can it really relate to accepting God into your life when you are ready? Wasn't there any time when you didn't have God in your life and then asked for him to come into your life and your life changed?

A. This question confuses the Sacrament of Confirmation with what some call "baptism in the Spirit". The two are totally different; hopefully we will have experienced both, so let's discuss both.

Confirmation confers the courage and gifts of the Holy Spirit that we need to be witnesses to Christ in our daily lives. In Acts 1:8, Jesus promised the Apostles that he would give them what they needed to combat the fears they had about serving Him, and in Acts 2:1-2, we hear of the birth of the Church at Pentecost when the Holy Spirit came upon them and gave them that strength. Jesus fulfills His promise to the Apostles in us today in the Sacrament of Confirmation. The Apostles had Jesus as a part of their daily lives for a long time, and their lives had certainly changed prior to that day at Pentecost. They had some years before they accepted Jesus into their lives and had witnessed the effect of that decision. In the coming of the Holy Spirit on this occasion the conviction of their faith was strengthened, and they were able to confront the opposition they met, an opposition which resulted in martyrdom; as it did for thirty-one of the first thirty-two popes.

There are several instances in Holy Scripture where the laying on of hands is described such as Acts 8:14-17 NIV:

> "When the apostles in Jerusalem heard that Samaria had accepted the word of God, they sent Peter and John to Samaria. When they arrived, they prayed for the new believers there that they might receive the Holy Spirit, because the Holy Spirit had not yet come upon any of them; they had simply been baptized into the name of the Lord Jesus. Then Peter and John placed their hands on them, and they received the Holy Spirit."

There is a close connection between Baptism and Confirmation as is evidenced in Hebrews 6:2. This connection is so close in fact that the early Christians normally conferred these two Sacraments during the same rite (they still do in Eastern Rite Catholic and Orthodox celebration of the rites). In truth, the Holy Spirit is given in both rites, but the function of the Holy Spirit in each is different. In Baptism, we are made members of Christ's Body, but in Confirmation we are given the power of God to bear fruit in our Christian life and to draw others into the Church. Because this bearing of fruit requires some maturity, the Latin Rite Catholic Church has chosen to confer this sacrament at an age in which maturity is evident. Confirmation, like Baptism, imprints on the soul an indelible spiritual mark, and for this reason, it cannot be repeated.

"Baptism in the Spirit" takes many forms and has different effects from one person to another. It can manifest itself at a definite moment in the form of a conscious moment, or it can be hidden and only gradually be made aware to the recipient and those around him/her. "Baptism in the Spirit" can happen several times to a person at different ages as different manifestations become evident.

We should always be eager to encounter the power and love of God in our lives, not only sacramentally but spiritually as well.

Recommended Reading:

Catechism of the Catholic Church, Libreria Editrice Vaticana, 1994, paras. 1212, 1285-1321.

EUCHARIST

Q. Why do you believe that the Eucharist is the Body and Blood of Christ?

Q. Where is the proof of the Eucharist in the Bible?

A. As I have said before, you cannot use the Bible to "prove" anything to those who choose not to believe. That said, there are many passages which show the Eucharist to be much more than a symbol very clearly.

The first place to look is John 6:25-71 where Jesus promises the Eucharist. This account, which occupies 2/3 of the chapter, describes Jesus' exchange with a crowd of disciples; probably numbering several thousand as this event follows the feeding of the 5,000 (most of the preceding part of the chapter), and these disciples have followed Him seeking more of this miraculous bread. After all, Moses provided bread for those who followed him during their wanderings in the desert. Jesus tells them that He is the bread of life that came down from heaven and those who come to Him will never be hungry. The disciples do not understand and grumbled because Jesus has said that He comes down from heaven, but they know that He is a man; they know His parents. Jesus again tells them that He is the living bread which came down from heaven and anyone who eats this bread will have eternal life. The disciples understand Him literally and begin to dispute among themselves because they don't understand how He can give them His flesh to eat. Jesus then underscores this literal interpretation by stating four times (in four successive verses, 53-56) that they must eat His Flesh and drink His Blood, or they will not have everlasting life. The Greek verb used in these four verses for "eat" is much stronger than the verb used earlier in His discourse; in this case it literally means "chew, gnaw"; hardly a word to be taken symbolically. Jesus then tells the disciples that the "Spirit gives life, the flesh counts for nothing". In other words, stop worrying about food for your flesh and start worrying about food for your Spirit (notice that he talks about "the flesh" and not "My flesh"; He is talking about the flesh of John 3:6). Then many of His disciples left Him. This is the only place in Holy Scripture where people cease to follow Him for a reason of doctrine. They have understood Him literally, and He, who understands perfectly, does not seek to change or modify their understanding; because there is no misunderstanding. Jesus then asks His apostles if they wish to leave too, but Peter, speaking for the rest, tells Him that although they don't understand, they will continue to follow Him because they know that He has been sent by God for their salvation. It is interesting to note that this is the first time in the Bible where it is noted that Judas Iscariot will later leave to betray Him (Judas didn't believe that Jesus could give His Flesh to eat and His Blood to drink and so left at the Last Supper when the Eucharist was instituted).

The second place to look is one of the Gospel accounts of the Last Supper so let's turn to Mark 14:17-26. This account is where the promise of John 6 to give His Body and Blood is fulfilled and it starts off by pointing out that Judas will leave to betray Him, the second time in the Bible that Judas' betrayal is mentioned. During the Passover liturgy the presiding elder explains the significance of the elements. Following this custom Jesus takes the bread, and later the cup, and after giving thanks (the Greek word is "eucharisteo") departs from the customary significance and instead says, *this is My Body. … this is My Blood.* When God speaks, what He pronounces comes into being (God said, "Let there be light …"). He then says that His Blood is the blood of the covenant which is poured out for many. This is the only time in Jesus' recorded life where He uses the word "covenant"; a word which when used in the Jewish liturgical sense, means the forming of an irrevocable sacred family bond. Just as during the original Passover the blood marked the homes of the members of God's family, so now, drinking His Blood marks the members of His family.

The third place to look is 1 Corinthians 10:16-17 where St. Paul tells us that when we partake of the bread and the cup we participate in the Body and Blood of Our Lord and that we are united because we all eat of the same loaf which is Christ. It is awfully hard to "partake of" and "participate in" something which is only figurative rather than real.

The final place to look is 1 Corinthians 11:23-30. Here, St. Paul reminds us that although he was not present at the Last Supper, he received revelation directly from the Lord. St. Paul then gives us the same account of the happenings at the Last Supper with the clarification from Jesus to "do this in remembrance of Me". Remembrance for a Jew is a lot more than looking back fondly on a past event. When a remembrance (memorial) sacrifice is offered, the participants are made present at the original event and participate in that event. Here, Jesus is telling His apostles to institute a perpetual memorial sacrifice for Him. St. Paul then goes on to warn the Corinthians, most of whom believe that the Eucharist is truly the Body and Blood of Christ, that they are to exclude themselves from participation in the meal if they do not recognize that it is the real presence of the Lord, or they will eat and drink damnation upon themselves. These words would not have been spoken, because there would be no need for the warning, if the Eucharist were a mere symbol.

Does this "prove" the Eucharist? It convinces me, because I have only three choices:

1. It is true;
2. The Bible is wrong; or
3. Jesus lied. Of the three choices, only the first one is acceptable.

<u>Recommended Reading:</u>

Catechism of the Catholic Church, Libreria Editrice Vaticana, 1994, paras. 1322-1419.

Currie, David B., *Born Fundamentalist, Born Again Catholic,* Ignatius Press, San Francisco, CA 94122, 1996, pp. 35-49.

Staples, Tim, "How to Explain the Eucharist", *Catholic Digest,* St. Paul, MN 55164, September 1997, pp. 75-78.

Hahn, Scott & Suprenant, Leon J. (Editors), *Catholic for a Reason,* Emmaus Road Press, 1998, pp. 159-180.

Q. When you go to Communion are you completely saved through Christ?

A. Reception of the Eucharist in a worthy manner makes us one with Christ. As such we have a pledge of heavenly bliss and of the future resurrection of our body. Jesus said in John 6:56 KJV:

> "'He that eateth my flesh, and drinketh my blood, dwelleth in me, and I in him.'"

By having Jesus dwell in us, He feeds our soul and increases its supernatural life by reinforcing the power of our will so we can withstand the temptations of sin. By receiving the Eucharist in a worthy manner, our soul is purged of the venial sins. If we were to die before we commit any sins after worthy reception of the Eucharist, we would be saved. It is our responsibility to avoid sin and having received the Eucharist in a worthy manner, we are strengthened to avoid sins in the future as we journey down the path toward our salvation.

Recommended Reading:

Catechism of the Catholic Church, Libreria Ed Editrice Vaticana, 1994, paras. 1391-1401,1407, 1416.

Ott, Dr. Ludwig, *Fundamentals of Catholic Dogma,* TAN Books and Publishers, Rockford, IL 61105, 1974, pp. 394-396.

Q. Why do we receive Communion?

A. Aside from the reasons cited in the answer to the preceding question (being united with Christ, receiving supernatural life for our soul and reinforced power to resist sin for our will, being purged of venial sin) the only other reason is because Jesus told us to, and we are obedient. We must always remember that each time we receive Holy Communion we receive God's graces, and the more grace we receive the easier it is to resist the temptations of sin.

Q. Is a person who doesn't believe that the Eucharist is truly the Body, Blood, Soul, and Divinity of Jesus really a Catholic?

A. No, they are not. Although we may not understand the doctrines of the Catholic Church, we must accept them. The Catholic faith is not a cafeteria style faith where we can go down the line of dogmas taking some of this, some of that, a double portion of something else, and avoiding the things we don't like. There are many things about which we do have a choice as to whether to accept them or not (for example, Marian apparitions and devotion to the Sacred Heart), but the Real Presence of Jesus in the Eucharist is not among them.

Examples of dogmas (those truths that the Catholic Church requires the faithful to accept as doctrine revealed by God), although not by any means a complete list, are: the divinity of Christ, the Blessed Trinity, the Real Presence of Christ in the Eucharist, the Immaculate Conception, and the bodily Assumption of the Blessed Virgin Mary.

Recommended Reading:

Catechism of the Catholic Church, Libreria Editrice Vaticana, 1994, paras. 88-94.

PENANCE/RECONCILIATION/ CONFESION

Q. What is Penance?

A. There are two paths which lead to heaven, which is our final goal. Both paths were given to us by Jesus in His infinite mercy. The first path is that of innocence: When we were baptized, the stain of original sin and all our individual sins were washed away, and we became absolutely pure in God's eyes. If we have been able to retain that baptismal innocence, avoiding even the slightest sin, this is the path by which we will enter heaven. Those of us who have not retained our baptismal innocence, who have stained our white baptismal garment by sin, must follow the second path, the path of penance. Through the Sacrament of Penance those who fall into sin after baptism are restored to God's grace.

Penance is not only receiving God's forgiveness; it is also an instrument of reconciliation with our brothers and sisters. The goal of this Sacrament is conversion and change in our lives. In this respect, the Sacrament of Penance is one of the most powerful – potentially the most powerful – instruments in the Church for spiritual growth and continuing conversion in our lives. God loves us always and will always forgive us, but we must respond to the message Jesus gave us:

> "The kingdom of God is near. Repent and believe the good news!" (Mark 1:15 NIV).

A significant part of that message of good news is the commandment to love one another, to be reconciled with our brother (Matthew 5:23-24).

Recommended Reading:
Catechism of the Catholic Church, Libreria Editrice Vaticana, 1994, paras. 1422-1498.

Q. Why do you have confession?

A. We have confession because we are sincerely sorry for our sins against God and our brothers and sisters. The Gospels tell us that when Jesus walked this earth, not only did He forgive people of their sins, He told them that they were forgiven. If He had not told them so, they would not have had certainty that their sins had, in fact, been forgiven. After His death and Resurrection, on that first Easter Sunday, the first commission that Jesus specifically gave to his Apostles was the responsibility and authority to forgive men's sins:

> "Again Jesus said, 'Peace be with you! As the Father has sent me, I am sending you.' And with that he breathed on them and said, 'Receive the Holy Spirit. If you forgive anyone's sins, their sins are forgiven; if you do not forgive them, they are not forgiven.'" (John 20:21-23 NIV).

How was Jesus sent? With full power and authority from His Father to bring about reconciliation between mankind and God, including the power to forgive individual sins. Jesus has begun the process of reconciliation and has appointed individuals to continue His work as His ambassadors. How are they to know which sins to forgive and which to retain? They must hear them in order to decide. The person seeking forgiveness will know that they have been forgiven when they have been told by Jesus' ambassadors, the priests.

Q. Why do you confess sins to a priest?
Q. Why must we confess our sins to a priest, and how can he forgive us our sins?
Q. If Jesus will forgive the truly repentant, why confess to a priest?

A. Our sins are confessed to a priest because that's the way the Bible tells us that our sins are forgiven by God. In the answer to the preceding question, we saw that Jesus commissioned the Apostles with the authority and responsibility to forgive sins. When they forgave sins, it wasn't they who were doing the forgiving, it was Jesus:

> "He that heareth you heareth me, and he that despiseth you despiseth me; and he that despiseth me despiseth him that sent me." (Luke 10:16 KJV).

Of the fact that this authority and responsibility was passed on to others by the Apostles is not in question because we are told:

> "Is any one of you sick? Let them call the elders of the church to pray over him and anoint him with oil in the name of the Lord. And the prayer offered in faith will make the sick person well; the Lord will raise him up. If they have sinned, they will be forgiven." (James 5:14-15 NIV).

This is what we call the Sacrament of the Anointing of the Sick for those with a physical illness but the next verse clarifies this even more. The next verse starts with the word "therefore" which should cause us to look to see what it is "there for". It is providing a summary of the teaching just concluded:

> "Therefore confess your sins to each other and pray for each other so that you may be healed. The prayer of righteous man is powerful and effective." (James 5:16 NIV).

Who are these "each other?" None other than the sick person and the elder of the church (some translations use "presbyter" rather than elder, the Greek is "presbyteros" from which the word "priest" is derived). When the spiritually ill, those who have sinned, confess their sins to the priest, the sins are forgiven and the healing process begins.

<u>Recommended Reading:</u>

Catechism of the Catholic Church, Libreria Editrice Vaticana, 1994, paras. 1461-1467.

Drummey, James J., *Catholic Replies,* C. R. Publications, Norwood, MA 02062, 1995, pp. 196-197.
Rumble, Rev. Dr. Leslie & Carty, Rev. Charles Mortimer, *Radio Replies, First Volume,* TAN Books & Publishers, Rockford, IL 61105, 1979, paras. 824-840.

Q. If you truly believe Jesus is present in the Eucharist, why do you have to see a priest for confession and why can't we confess to Jesus in Adoration?
Q. Why can't I pray to God for forgiveness instead of telling a priest?

A. Because that's not the way that Jesus Himself set it up. His first act on that first Easter Sunday was to tell His Apostles that He wanted them to forgive men's sins and to give them the power and authority to do so in His Name (John 20:19-23). If we are truly His followers, we must do exactly what He tells us to do. He makes the rules, we simply obey.

Q. Not married in the church. Want to go to confession.

A. Surprising as it may sound, anyone can go to confession. Only Catholics who are willing to try to overcome their sinful nature can receive absolution. For all others, including Protestants, a meeting with the priest (and Christ) in the confessional can be a very valuable counseling session which will begin to re-order their lives.

Q. Some churches have group confessions. Since you are the only priest and seem to be overworked, why not give it a try? Is group confession legal?

A. Group confessions with general absolution without private confession are not to be performed except in cases where there is imminent danger of death or in serious necessity (such as members of the military who are going to a battle zone). The diocesan bishop is to decide when these conditions are present. The law of the Church (Canons 962 and 963 of the *1983 Code of Canon Law*) says that anyone who has received absolution in this manner must go to private confession as soon as possible thereafter and may not receive general absolution again until after they have confessed their sins privately.

<u>Recommended Reading:</u>

Stravinskas, Rev. Peter M. J., *The Catholic Answer Book 2,* Our Sunday Visitor, Huntington, IN 46750, 1994, pp. 154-155.

Q. What is the meaning of "Christ died for our sins?"

A. It is true that Jesus died for our sins (1 Corinthians 15:3). It is also true that Jesus bore our sins in His body on the cross so we might die to sin and live to righteousness (1 Peter 2:24). When we read these verses without the benefit of an Old Testament understanding of what is being addressed, we misunderstand the covenant discipline of suffering.

Since the sin of Adam and Eve, the sin of disobedience, heaven was closed to humanity:

> "After he drove man out, he placed on the east side of the Garden of Eden Cherubim and a flaming sword flashing back and forth to guard the way to the tree of life." (Genesis 3:24).

Even though heaven was closed, God still communicated directly with His creation. However, since the sin of the golden calf, God's chosen people were no longer treated as part of His family, but rather as His servants or slaves; he no longer communicated with them directly but through intermediaries (Exodus 33:3). In both cases, the reason for the estrangement was that mankind had so strained their covenant family relationship with God that the punitive curses associated with the covenant had come into play. Because of the sin of Adam and Eve, suffering entered into the world; fruit-bearing became painful, both in giving birth and working to provide for the family (Genesis 3:16). Because of the sin of the golden calf, no longer was the firstborn of the family the priest of the family, now only Levites were priests (Exodus 32:28-29), and bloody sacrifices were required in order to approach God (Leviticus 1:2). These sacrifices were public, costly, and ineffective.

When we say, "Christ died for our sins", we are not talking necessarily about the sins we personally commit as we live our lives, but the sins of humanity; of Adam and Eve, of the Israelites. The sins which estranged God's creation from Him. Jesus did what Adam should have done; He obeyed His Father. In Jesus' passion He suffered in a garden, His brow sweating blood, and on the cross, He wore the crown of thorns, which grew in the ground cursed because of Adam's sin. In His death upon the cross Jesus, our High Priest, entered the heavenly tabernacle and offered His own Body as the perfect sacrifice to atone for the separation caused by the golden calf. In Exodus 26, God told Moses to make a curtain and place the Tabernacle behind it, and no one, except the High Priest, could go past the curtain. This sacrifice of self-donating love opened heaven,

> "…for the sun stopped shining. And the curtain of the temple was torn in two." (Luke 23:45);

and this made it possible for us to have our sins forgiven,

> "Again Jesus said, 'Peace be with you! As the Father has sent me, I am sending you.' And with that he breathed on them and said, 'Receive the Holy Spirit. If you forgive anyone's sins, their sins are forgiven; if you do not forgive them, they are not forgiven.'" (John 20:21-23 NIV).

It is not a case of "Jesus did it all, there is nothing more I can do". Because of Jesus' sacrifice for our sins, He showed us that it is possible for us to obey God, to have our sins forgiven and enter heaven. He showed us self-donating love, how to suffer in a redemptive way, to make our death united with His and to bring grace to other people.

Recommended Reading:
Catechism of the Catholic Church, Libreria Editrice Vaticana, 1994, paras. 1499, 1521.

Q. When was mandatory confession started, and who did it?

A. As illustrated in the answer to an earlier question in this chapter where James 5:14-15 was discussed, Confession has been mandatory since Jesus instituted the Sacrament. In fact, in the early Church, sins were confessed to the presbyter (priest/bishop/elder) in front of the entire congregation. It wasn't until around the 5th century that private, rather than public, confession became the norm. The Fourth Lateran Council (1215) ordered annual reception of Penance and the Eucharist. The Council of Trent (1545-1563) required confession of the kind and number of sins.

Q. When was the last time you went to confession?

A. The frequency of visitation to the Sacrament of Confession is a highly personal matter between the penitent and God. This is not the type of question which any person is obligated to answer in any manner other than as stated in the first sentence. This said, if you wish to disclose the frequency of your visitation to this Sacrament you may do so.

SACRAMENT OF THE SICK

Q. What is Anointing of the Sick?

A. The Sacrament of the Anointing of the Sick is the second of two healing ministries which Jesus gave to His Church, the first being the Sacrament of Penance. This sacrament is based upon James 5:14-15 KJV where Jesus says:

> "'Is any sick among you? let him call for the elders of the church; and let them pray over him, anointing him with oil in the name of the Lord: And the prayer of faith shall save the sick, and the Lord shall raise him up; and if he have committed sins, they shall be forgiven him.'"

In ancient times, no sharp distinction was made between physical health and spiritual health; those who were physically ill suffered mentally as well and those who suffered from guilt or depression often displayed physical symptoms too. The same is true today. In fact, the word "salvation" is derived from the Latin "salus" which means "health." Jesus restored health to the body and to the soul when He walked this earth, and left His Church the ability to do likewise as it carries on His ministry; Acts 9:34 for instance tells of Peter healing in Jesus' name.

A few years ago, this Sacrament was called "Extreme Unction" and was administered only when the recipient was thought to be dying. At that time, it was part of the last rites for the dying: making one's last Confession, receiving one's last Communion (Viaticum), and receiving one's final Anointing. Since the Second Vatican Council, the emphasis of this Sacrament has been changed from that of the dying, to those in serious need. Thus, anyone who is going to have an operation or who is advanced in years can request the Sacrament. This Sacrament can be repeated as illness worsens or new disabilities manifest themselves.

Recommended Reading:
Catechism of the Catholic Church, Libreria Editrice Vaticana, 1994, paras. 1499-1532.

Q. If a person has not been to Church or practiced his faith for many years, are they forgiven their sins on receiving the last rites?

A. The "last rites" (last Confession, last Eucharist, and last Anointing), like all Sacraments, are always effective. What impedes the effectiveness of the Sacraments is the disposition of the individual receiving them. If the person receiving the Sacraments is not truly repentant for their sins and open to God's forgiveness, that forgiveness is not forthcoming.

Recommended Reading:
Catechism of the Catholic Church, Libreria Editrice Vaticana, 1994, para. 1523.

Rumble, Rev. Dr. Leslie & Carty, Rev. Charles Mortimer, *Radio Replies, Third Volume,* TAN Books & Publishers, Rockford, IL 61105, 1979, paras. 908-911.

Q. What if there is no priest around when you die, and you don't get the last blessing?

A. God, in His infinite justice and mercy, always reads the disposition of the heart. If the individual was truly repentant for their sins and open to the effectiveness of the Sacraments, even though they were unable to receive them, their sins will be forgiven.

HOLY ORDERS

Q. Did Jesus establish the priesthood?

A. The first thing to remember is that Jesus came not to abolish the Law and the prophets (the Old Testament) but to fulfill them (Matthew 5:17). The Old Testament priesthood was one which had a high priest, other priests to assist him, and the laity for whom they performed their duties. The duties of the priests in the Old Testament might be most accurately described as one of offering sacrifice, making atonement, making access to God, and teaching (although much of the responsibility of teaching had been at least partially handed over to the scribes). The high priest was specifically charged with offering sacrifice for the people (Leviticus 16:15-34; and 24). The Old Testament (Covenant) sacrifices were ineffective, but this does not nullify the need for sacrifice in the New Covenant.

Jesus is our New Covenant high priest (Hebrews 4:14) and as high priest in heaven He offers His sacrifice in our behalf (Hebrews 5:1). Only in Jesus is the ultimate character of the priesthood fully revealed: He offered the sacrifice of His body on the altar of the cross once; He is continually making atonement for our sins through the continued presentation of His sacrifice to the Father (Revelation 5:6) thereby allowing us access to the Father. He also taught His Apostles, and He teaches us through His successors and those they appoint.

The Old Testament high priest had an ordained priesthood to assist him. When Jesus told His apostles at the last supper, "Do this in remembrance of me (Luke 22:19, KJV/NIV)", He was specifically directing (and ordaining) them to perform a particular Jewish priestly act: offer a memorial sacrifice. In this case, because only His own body is the sacrifice sufficient to open heaven, He has also told them, "This is my Body which is given for you (Luke 22:19, KJV)." He is not telling them to kill Him again, He is telling them to join in His once for all sacrifice (a Jewish memorial sacrifice made the participants present at the original event, even many generations later).

Like the Old Testament (Covenant) laity who brought their sacrifices to the altar, all New Covenant believers share, in some measure, in the priesthood of Jesus. We have realized the blessings of the Covenant that God made with the Israelites at Mount Sinai; we are a royal priesthood, a chosen people, a holy nation, a people belonging to God (Exodus 19:56; 1 Peter 2:9). But the sacrificial requirement of the priesthood was not done away with, even for us, when the New Covenant was instituted. This is why we are told to offer ourselves as a living sacrifice, holy and pleasing to God (Romans 12:1).

Preaching (teaching) was (and is) only one small part of the duties of a priest. Teaching is also one of the gifts of the Holy Spirit which is given to members of Christ' s Body, the Church (not just those who are ordained) (1 Corinthians 12:28-29). The ordained priest's primary responsibility is to offer the memorial sacrifice of Jesus in order to make Him present for us so that we can join in His covenant relationship with God the Father. The great commission to baptize and teach (in that order) (Matthew

28:19-20), to which the questioner refers was given to the eleven first, but as disciples, it is also the commission of every follower (that's what "disciple" means) of Jesus (this is why any person can baptize if an ordained priest or deacon is not available).

Recommended Reading:

Catechism of the Catholic Church, Libreria Editrice Vaticana, 1994, paras. 1536-1600.

Q. Were priests ever allowed to marry?

A. In the early Church, priests were allowed to marry. Tertullian writes in 213 A.D., "Peter alone [among the Apostles] do I find married, and through mention of his mother-in-law. I presume he was a monogamist; for the Church, built upon him, would for the future appoint to every degree of orders none but monogamists. As for the rest [of the Apostles], since I do not find them married, I must presume that they were either eunuchs or continent." Since the Second Lateran Council (1139 A.D.) all candidates for priestly ordination in the Latin Rite have been required to take the vow of celibacy. To this day, married men in the Eastern rites of the Catholic Church (Uinates, Marionites, etc.) are allowed to be ordained (once they are ordained, an Eastern rite priest cannot marry even if widowed). No married Eastern rite priest can be ordained a bishop. The Orthodox Church has the same rules as the Eastern Rite Catholics.

As far back as the second century there is a strong endorsement of celibacy as the Apostolic Constitutions state, "If a Priest or Deacon is not already married, he can never contract marriage."

Recommended Reading:

Catechism of the Catholic Church, Libreria Editrice Vaticana, 1994, para. 1580.

Rumble, Rev, Dr. Leslie & Carty, Rev. Charles Mortimer, *Radio Replies, First Volume,* TAN Books & Publishers, Rockford, IL 61105, 1979, paras. 1193-1195.

Q. If the Church is experiencing a shortage of vocations, why will it not consider allowing priests to marry?
Q. Why don't priests get married?
Q. Why can't priests marry, but an Episcopal priest can marry and then become a Catholic married priest?

A. The celibate priesthood is a rule of the Latin Rite of the Catholic Church. As a rule, rather than dogma, it could be changed. Such a change is unlikely in the foreseeable future, even with a shortage of vocations in Europe and North America, as numerous vocations are coming from Africa and Asia. It may be that those countries who once provided foreign missionaries will be on the receiving end from the countries which they evangelized.

The rule of celibacy is based on the example set by Jesus and on the teachings of Saints Matthew and Paul:

> "For there are some eunuchs, which were so born from their mother's womb: and there are some eunuchs, which were made eunuchs of men: and there be eunuchs, which have made themselves eunuchs for the kingdom of heaven's sake. He that is able to receive it, let him receive it." (Matthew 19:12 KJV);

> "Now concerning the things whereof ye wrote unto me: It is good for a man not to touch a woman. Nevertheless, to avoid fornication, let every man have his own wife, and let every woman have her own husband. ... For I would that all men were even as I myself. But every man hath his proper gift of God, one after this manner, and another after that. I say therefore to the unmarried and widows, it is good for them if they abide even as I. But if they cannot contain, let them marry: for it is better to marry than to burn. And unto the married I command, yet not I, but the Lord, Let not the wife depart from her husband: But and if she depart, let her remain unmarried or be reconciled to her husband: and let not the husband put away his wife. ... But I would have you without carefulness. He that is unmarried careth for the things that belong to the Lord, how he may please the Lord: But he that is married careth for the things that are of the world, how he may please his wife. There is difference also between a wife and a virgin. The unmarried woman careth for the things of the Lord, that she may be holy both in body and in spirit: but she that is married careth for the things of the world, how she may please her husband." (1 Corinthians 7:2, 7-11, 32-34 KJV)

There are those who say, "It is not natural for a priest not to be married." To them I would reply, "You are quite correct; it is not natural - it is supernatural. It takes a supernatural grace to live the celibate life. A grace that only God can give."

As to those clergy from other denominations who convert and choose the Catholic priesthood as their vocation, each case is reviewed individually by the Holy See in Rome before an exception to the rule is granted. This exception allows them, although married, to receive priestly ordination in the Latin Rite, but if their wife dies, they must then live a celibate life.

Recommended Reading:
Catechism of the Catholic Church, Libreria Editrice Vaticana, 1994, para. 1579.

Q. Why no woman priests? I'm very happy to see girls on the altar, why aren't women allowed to preach?
Q. Were there ever woman priests?

A. There have never been woman priests in the Church founded by Christ. There were priestesses in the pagan religions which abounded at the time of Christ. There have been women who claimed to be priests, even in the early Church. Of these Tertullian writes:

> "And the heretical women themselves, how shameless are they! They make bold to teach, to debate, to work exorcisms, to undertake cures, and perhaps even to baptize. Their ordinations are casual, capricious, and changeable." (*Demurrer Against the Heretics*, 41,5-6, 200 A.D.).

The prohibition against women preaching can be found in 1 Timothy 2:12 KJV:

> "But I suffer not a woman to teach, nor to usurp authority over the man, but to be in silence.";

And also, in 1 Corinthians 14:34-35 KJV:

> "Let your women keep silence in the churches: for it is not permitted unto them to speak; but they are commanded to be under obedience, as also saith the law. And if they will learn any thing, let them ask their husbands at home: for it is a shame for women to speak in the church."

As chauvinistic as this sounds in our liberated modem world, women were not allowed to speak in the synagogue in Jesus' time and He, who was not afraid to correct any impropriety in God's eyes, never spoke against this practice and His Apostles followed His example. Neither did He choose a woman to be one of His Apostles. As Pope John Paul II said in his Apostolic Letter *Ordinatio Sacerdotalis* (May 1994):

> "In order that all doubt may be removed regarding a matter of great importance, a matter which pertains to the Church's divine constitution itself, in virtue of my ministry of confirming the brethren (cf. Luke 22:32) I declare that the Church has no authority whatsoever to confer priestly ordination on women and that this judgement is to be definitively held by all the Church's faithful."

Q. What is a deacon, and what is his function?

A. A deacon is an ordained member of the clergy with limited faculties. He cannot, for example, confect the Eucharist, hear confessions, or administer the Sacrament of the Sick. The deacon's job is that of service to the bishop and priests in the celebration of the divine mysteries, above all the Holy Eucharist, in the distribution of Holy Communion, in assisting at the blessing of marriages, in the proclamation of the Gospel and preaching, in presiding over funerals, and in dedicating themselves to the various ministries of charity. Deacons are ordained "to the bishop" and, like priests, are assigned by the bishop to the parishes they serve. Deacons can be the only witness and representative of the Church at a wedding and weddings so performed are as lawful and legal as those performed by a priest or minister. Likewise, a deacon can perform a Sacramental Baptism for which a baptismal certificate is issued.

Recommended Reading:

Catechism of the Catholic Church, Libreria Editrice Vaticana, 1994, paras. 1569-1571.

Q. The 11 Apostles I remember, but the 7 Deacons I don't recall.

A. The origin of the diaconate can be found in Acts 6:1-6, where the seven first deacons are named.

MATRIMONY

Q. Why does the Church oppose divorce?

A. Civil divorce by itself is not the problem. The problem occurs when remarriage takes place. In the Holy Scriptures, we read:

> "'Haven't you read,' he [Jesus] replied, 'that at the beginning the Creator, made them male and female,' and said, 'For this reason a man will leave his father and mother and be united to his wife, and the two will become one flesh?' So they are no longer two, but one flesh. Therefore what God has joined together, let man not separate.' 'Why then,' they asked, 'did Moses command that a man give his wife a certificate of divorce and send her away?' Jesus replied, 'Moses permitted you to divorce your wives because your hearts were hard. But it was not this way from the beginning. I tell you that anyone who divorces his wife, except for sexual immorality, and marries another woman commits adultery.'" (Matthew 19:4-9 NIV)

> "They said, 'Moses permitted a man to write a certificate of divorce and send her away.' 'It was because your hearts were hard that Moses wrote you this law,' Jesus replied. 'But at the beginning of creation God made them male

> and female. For this reason a man will leave his father and mother and be united to his wife, and the two will become one flesh. So they are no longer two, but one flesh. Therefore what God has joined together, let man not separate.' … 'Anyone who divorces his wife and marries another woman commits adultery against her. And if she divorces her husband and marries another man, she commits adultery.'" (Mark 10:4-9, 11-12 NIV)

> "Anyone who divorces his wife and marries another woman commits adultery, and the man who marries a divorced woman commits adultery." (Luke 16:18 NIV)

The Church does not permit divorce. God who does not permit divorce. He has revealed this through the mouth of His Son. This does not mean that a man and a woman must live together in an abusive relationship. The Church recognizes that there are situations where physical, emotional or spiritual harm may come to a partner if they remain under the same roof. The Church, in these cases, recommends and supports separation of bed and board for the individuals involved. This separation may even take the form of a civil divorce, but remarriage is forbidden as they are still married in the eyes of God.

Recommended Reading:

Catechism of the Catholic Church, Libreria Editrice Vaticana, 1994, paras. 1601-1666.

Rumble, Rev. Dr. Leslie & Carty, Rev. Charles Mortimer, *Radio Replies, First Volume,* TAN Books & Publishers, Rockford, IL 61105, 1979, paras. 889-890, 892-895.

Q. Is a second marriage breaking a Commandment or breaking a law of the Church?

A. As we saw in the answer to the preceding question, it is breaking a Commandment. Those involved in the second marriage are breaking the sixth one (the seventh as Protestants number them): "You shall not commit adultery."

Q. On the question of divorce, Jesus said there was only one exception: Lewd conduct or sins of chastity. Why does the Church not honor these words of Christ?

A. This "exception" is in Matthew 19:9, but it really isn't an exception. If one reads this verse carefully, paying special attention to the punctuation, you will notice that although divorce may be allowed for marital unfaithfulness (the Greek word is "pornea"); remarriage, even in the case of this "exception", is not allowed. If remarriage were allowed, the exception clause would be located after the statement about remarriage rather than before it. Again, the problem is not with the divorce, but the remarriage.

<u>Recommended Reading:</u>

Rumble, Rev. Dr. Leslie & Carty, Rev. Charles Mortimer, *Radio Replies, First Volume,* TAN Books & Publishers, Rockford, IL 61105, 1979, paras. 892-895.

Q. Can a person who was married in Church and got a divorce, and then got married again, and when the second husband died married for a third time, receive Communion after the first husband has died? Can I receive Communion now?

A. It would appear that the physical impediments to having your (third) wedding blessed by the Church have been removed, at least on your side of the marriage. If this is your current husband's first marriage, then all impediments may well have been removed. I would recommend that you make an appointment with your parish priest to discuss your situation and receive absolution if it is your sincere desire to return to full communion with the Church.

Q. Is someone who was married to a non-Catholic in the Church, considered married in the eyes of the Church?

A. Any marriage witnessed by the Church is valid in the eyes of the Church. In fact, any first marriage between baptized non-Catholics performed in any Christian setting is presumed to be valid by the Catholic Church until a decree of nullity is obtained.

<u>Recommended Reading:</u>

Catechism of the Catholic Church, Libreria Editrice Vaticana, 1994, paras. 1633-1637, 1640.

Q. Please explain annulments.

Q. How is it possible for Catholics to be married in the Church 2 or 3 times while their ex's are still alive?

A. An annulment (decree of nullity) is a finding by the Church that a sacramental (as opposed to civil) marriage never existed, therefore the parties were never married in the eyes of God. There are many things which could contribute to finding a marriage null such as coercion or grave external fear (a shotgun wedding for instance), lack of consent due to the mental instability of one of the parties, lack of consent because one of the parties considered marriage to be a legal short-term relationship which could be abandoned at will, or lack of consummation.

Recommended Reading:

Catechism of the Catholic Church, Libreria Editrice Vaticana, 1994, paras. 1625-1632.

Rumble, Rev. Dr. Leslie & Carty, Rev. Charles Mortimer, *Radio Replies, First Volume,* TAN Books & Publishers, Rockford, IL 61105, 1979, paras. 897-905.

Q. Does an annulment make your children illegitimate in the Church?

A. No. Legitimacy and illegitimacy are legal terms applied by the secular world to children born in or out of the bounds of a civil marriage. All children are legitimate in the eyes of God or He would not have created them.

MISCELLANEOUS

Q. Why doesn't the church pay taxes and owns so much land?

A. The payment or nonpayment of taxes by the Church (and all other nonprofit charitable organizations) is a matter which is decided by each individual nation. In the case of the United States, the Congress decided that all religious institutions (Protestant, Catholic, Mormon, Jewish, Hindu, etc.) would be exempt from the payment of taxes on those of their holdings which were used for religious purposes. Activities and holdings not of a strictly religious nature (such as owning and/or operating a winery or book publishing enterprise for instance) are taxed.

Q. What does spirituality mean to you?

Q. How has spirituality influenced the actions that you participate in?

A. Spirituality is not something which is different from "real life". Rather, it is purposefully becoming aware that God is all around us. It is easy to be aware of God's presence when we are comfortable with our situation: when things are going well. It is sometimes very difficult to be aware of God's presence when we are experiencing difficulties, especially of the gut-wrenching variety.

Awareness of God's nearness is not something which most of us are born with. Instead, it is something which we have to work on and develop. God is always there but our being able to discern His presence is something which takes practice. Like sports, the more you do it the better you get at it. But even some of our most well-known saints experienced periods of spiritual dryness; times when prayer and contemplation were difficult. It was during these times that they worked the hardest on their relationship with God. When we experience such a period of spiritual dryness, it is time for us, like the Saints, to return to the basics, to concentrate on placing the Eucharist near to the center of our life. Frequent Communion and prayer before the Blessed Sacrament will provide the focus necessary to discern God's presence, first in the Eucharist, and then in our lives. Once that awareness is enkindled, we can connect our inner life to our outer one and become whole; one body and spirit striving to do God's will in our everyday lives.

Q. What are some things that we have in common with other religions?

A. This is such a broad question it is quite difficult to answer. If you are asking about religions such as Buddhism, Muslim, Shintoism, Christianity and Judaism, the commonality doesn't extend much beyond the belief in the existence of a Supreme Being. If you are asking about different Christian faiths such as Lutheranism, Methodism, Baptist, Catholicism and Presbyterianism there are many more common beliefs such as the Blessed Trinity, the necessity of Baptism, and the efficacy of Jesus' sacrifice.

Recommended Reading:

Catoir, John T., *World Religions; Beliefs Behind Today's Headlines,* The Christophers, New York, NY 10017, 1992.

Mead, Frank S., *Handbook of Denominations in The United States,* Abingdon Press, Nashville, TN, 1983.

Whalen, William J., *Separated Brethren,* Our Sunday Visitor, Huntington, IN 46750, 1979.

Q. Were some of the truths revealed by the 2nd Vatican Council misrepresented by liberal priests in America?

A. It seems as though there is misrepresentation by someone after almost every ecumenical council. In the case of Vatican II, because of the ready access to the media and the willingness of the media to engage in activities which cause discord (and therefore headlines), this misrepresentation has become much more visible. Vatican II, in fact, did not change any of the dogmas of the Catholic Church. Dogmas, by their very nature, are unchangeable. What was changed were some of the practices and like a pendulum the change went too far in one direction but is now returning to a more neutral position.

Recommended Reading:

Flannery, Austin, *Vatican Council II: The Conciliar and Post Conciliar Documents,* Costello Publishing Co., Northport, NY 11768, 1992.

Flannery, Austin, *Vatican Council II: More Post Conciliar Documents,* Costello Publishing Co., Northport, NY 11768, 1982.

Q. Why does the Church allow priests to disagree with the Pope on national TV?

A. The Church does not screen the remarks of their clergy before they are allowed to appear in public. It is up to the bishop to ensure that all official teaching of the Church within his diocese conforms to the teaching of the Magisterium. If the teaching does not conform, it is the responsibility of the bishop to correct it. In the case of some news accounts in recent years, the individual priest may in fact have been relieved of his clerical faculties by his bishop even though he is still a priest (because he was ordained "a priest forever according to the order of Melchizedek"). Such a person cannot function as a priest (say Mass, hear confessions, anoint the sick, etc.). That person is speaking as an individual and not as a representative of the clergy.

Q. Aren't Catholics who disagree with Church teachings really Protestants?

A. There are different degrees of disagreement. One can question whether or not a priest should be allowed to marry, whether or not communion should be taken in the hand, whether or not girls should be altar servers. These are all Church rules which are subject to change. When the questioning becomes a point of division within the Church community, it is no longer questioning but rebellion. Points of dogma may be questioned in order to gain a better understanding but never to effect change. The teachings of the Catholic Church are not like a menu where you can take some of this, some of that, a double helping of dessert, but no chastity or penance. Once a doctrine is knowingly rejected, the person is no longer a Catholic as they have excommunicated themselves.

Q. If a person is ignorant about Catholic doctrine is he really a Catholic?

A. If they have been baptized in the Catholic Church, they are Catholic even though they may not know or understand the doctrines of the Church. It is the duty of every Catholic to learn the truths of their faith. This can be done by attending Catholic Bible studies, seminars and retreats, and also by sitting in on R.C.I.A. classes.

Q. What must a person do (and believe) to be considered a Catholic by the Church?

A. First, they must be baptized. Second, they must accept the 10 Commandments as the model for their life. Third, they must subscribe to the beliefs expressed in the Apostles' Creed (or Nicene Creed). Finally, they must accept the dogmatic statements issued by the ecumenical councils and the popes as true and binding upon their faith. Obviously, all this doesn't happen all at once when an infant is baptized, but this is what is expected of an adult believer, whether they are a convert or a cradle Catholic. (See Apostles' Creed in Appendix.)

Q. What to tell someone that says that they do not go to church because of the changing rules and also because of what the priest said?

A. This is the same Church which Jesus Himself founded upon Peter, the rock. The people have never made the rules. The changing rules which people complain about are superficial in nature: how long to fast before receiving Holy Communion, whether to receive Holy Communion in the hand or on the tongue, whether the priest should face the people or not, whether girls should serve at the altar, etc. Those who complain about changes in the rules are most likely not really complaining about them but instead choosing to use them as an excuse for not participating in Mass. The problem is much deeper than rules. It instead revolves around whether the person is willing to do God's bidding rather than their own. The Catholic Church is not a democracy where we vote on what we want to do. It is a theocracy; run by God and those chosen by Him to do His Will.

As to what a priest has said there are three choices: the priest was in error, the listener misunderstood what the priest said, or the listener did not hear what they wanted to hear but instead heard what God wanted them to hear. In any case, the first response should be to make an appointment with the priest for a private discussion to ensure that what was heard was correctly understood. This done and satisfaction not having been attained, a discussion with the Vicar General for the diocese is in order, then, if necessary, a discussion with the bishop. Finally, an appeal can be made to the Papal Nuncio in Washington, D.C. The person making these appeals however must always be aware that they are not the final judge of what is right and what is wrong, and if they refuse to listen even to the Church, they should be treated as a pagan or a tax collector (Matthew 18:17).

Q. Why are Holy Days observed in some places and not in other places?

A. The National Council of Catholic Bishops for the United States has determined which days are holy days of obligation for the United States. Some of these days are different from those chosen by the Council of Catholic Bishops for Canada, or Mexico, or Ireland for example. Latin-rite Catholics in the United States observe more holy days than do Catholics in many other countries. The problem is determining which holy days are bound by which rules. Simply put, there are six holy days of obligation for most of the dioceses of the United States: Christmas (December 25), Mary Mother of God (January 1), Ascension (the sixth Thursday after Easter; but in some dioceses Ascension is moved to the 7th Sunday of Easter), Assumption (August 15), All Saints (November 1), and Immaculate Conception (December 8). But there are exceptions to the rules. When August 15, November 1 or January 1 fall on a Saturday or a Monday, the obligation to attend Mass is no longer in force. In nine western states, the feast of the Ascension has been transferred to the following Sunday. Catholics in Hawaii, following the practice of the neighbors in the South Pacific, observe all Sundays and two additional feasts, Christmas and the Immaculate Conception, as holy days of obligation

Q. Why did the Church mishandle pedophile priests so badly?

A. The Catholic Church as a whole did not mismanage the investigation and prosecution of pedophile priests, but some individuals and dioceses did. No matter what the intention of the persons involved in not pursuing the issue more vigorously and openly, failure to do so was wrong. Reasons given vary from not wanting to subject the Church to public scandal to not wanting to embarrass the priest involved and everything in between. As a result, the Church has been publicly ridiculed and the priesthood as a whole was embarrassed. As we have all learned, it is never allowable in God's eyes to commit a sin (or fail to admit that one has been committed) even if the attempted result is believed to be for the common good.

Q. I would like to have a clearer understanding of what the Church teaches as it pertains to capital punishment, especially execution.
Q. Can Catholics support the death penalty for murderers, rapists, and pedophiles?

A. If someone is causing harm to society, it is society's responsibility to render that individual incapable of inflicting further harm. The traditional teaching of the Church down through the ages has acknowledged the right and duty of legitimate public authority to punish malefactors proportionate to the gravity of the crime, not excluding, in cases of extreme gravity, the death penalty. However, we must also recognize that if incarceration is sufficient to defend the public against the individual malefactor, the public authority should limit itself to such means and ensure that the individual will not have their sentence reduced or otherwise be released to again become a threat to society. The ultimate judge is God, and He will give each individual their just reward. When we attempt to avenge the crime, we become no better than the original perpetrator.

Recommended Reading:

Catechism of the Catholic Church, Libreria Editrice Vaticana, 1994, paras. 2266-2267, 2306.

Q. We need to ask everyone to sing during Mass. We are praising God. God does not hear our singing if we don't sing.

A. How correct you are! The psalmist tells us:

> "Sing aloud unto God our strength: make a joyful noise unto the God of Jacob." (Psalm 81:1 KJV).

Notice that the psalmist doesn't say anything about being in tune. A congregation which sings earnestly never sounds out of tune, even if no one can carry a tune. As Saint Augustine said, "He who sings prays twice."

Recommended Reading:

Catechism of the Catholic Church, Libreria Editrice Vaticana, 1994, paras. 1156-1158.

APPENDIX

How was the Apostles' Creed formulated? It is said that the Blessed Virgin Mary appeared to Venerable Mary of Agreda (1602-1665) and told her how it came about. She reportedly reminded the Apostles that Jesus had emphasized to them that they all may be one in everything as He and the Father are one. This would include being one in preaching the truth. She asked each of the Apostles to define a mystery of the faith as the Holy Spirit inspired them. Peter began.

The Apostles' Creed	
I believe in God, the Father Almighty, Creator of heaven and earth.	St. Peter
And in Jesus Christ, His Only Son, Our Lord.	St. Andrew
Who was conceived by the Holy Spirit, born of the Virgin Mary.	St. James the Greater
Suffered under Pontius Pilate, was crucified, died and was buried.	St. John
He descended into hell, arose from the dead on the third day.	St. Thomas
He ascended into heaven and is seated at the right hand of God the Father almighty.	St. James the Less
From whence He shall come to judge the living and the dead.	St. Philip
I believe in the Holy Spirit.	St. Bartholomew
The Holy Catholic Church, the Communion of Saints.	St. Matthew
The Forgiveness of sins.	St. Simon
The Resurrection of the Body.	St. Thaddeus
And Life Everlasting.	St. Mathias
Amen. Venerable Mary Agreda	

From *The Whole Truth About the Catholic Church and the Holy Bible* by Fr. John Noone: The Council of Nicaea in 325 affirmed the equality and divinity of the Father and the Son. However, the Arian heresy continued. In 381, the Council of Constantinople I reaffirmed the teaching of Nicaea and taught the equality and divinity of the Holy Spirit also. The Council gave us the Nicene Creed which is said at Mass every Sunday in the Catholic Church. (https://frjohnnoonesbooks.wordpress.com/)

Updates to Recommended Reading:

1983 Code of Canon Law, https://www.vatican.va/archive/cod-iuris-canonici/cic_index_en.html

Catechism of the Catholic Church: https://www.vatican.va/archive/ENG0015/_INDEX.HTM

And https://scborromeo2.org/catechism-of-the-catholic-church

- *Catechism of the Catholic Church* - Table of Contents
- *Catechism of the Catholic Church* - Table of Contents with Paragraph Numbers
- *Catechism of the Catholic Church* - Index
- *Catechism of the Catholic Church* - Abbreviations
- How to Read the *Catechism of the Catholic Church*
- *Compendium of the Catechism of the Catholic Church* [on the Vatican's website]

Catholic Tracts, Catholic Answers, 2020 Gallespie Way, El Cajon, CA 92020, (888) 291-8000, https://www.catholic.com/tract

McNamara, Fr. Edward, "Extraordinary Form; Book of Blessings", A Zenit Daily Dispatch, Rome, 2 Nov. 2010 (Zenit), https://www.ewtn.com/catholicism/library/extraordinary-form-book-of-blessings-4549

Myers, Bishop John of Peoria, IL, (1 June 1990), *The Obligations of Catholics and the Rights of Unborn Children*, pastoral letter, https://www.rcan.org/june-1990

Pope John Paul II, *Evangelium Vitae* (The Gospel of Life), Encyclical Letter, March 25, 1995, https://www.vatican.va/content/john-paul-ii/en/encyclicals/documents/hf_jp-ii_enc_25031995_evangelium-vitae.html

Pope John Paul II, *Ordinatio Sacerdotalis* (May 1994), Apostolic Letter, https://www.vatican.va/content/john-paul-ii/en/apost_letters/1994/documents/hf_jp-ii_apl_19940522_ordinatio-sacerdotalis.html

Pope John Paul II, *Universi Dominici Gregis*, (Apostolic Constitution On the Vacancy of The Apostolic See and The Election of The Roman Pontiff), February 22, 1996, https://www.vatican.va/content/john-paul-ii/en/apost_constitutions/documents/hf_jp-ii_apc_22021996_universi-dominici-gregis.html

Pope Paul VI, *Humane Vitae,* Encyclical Letter 29 July 1968, https://www.vatican.va/content/paul-vi/en/encyclicals/documents/hf_p-vi_enc_25071968_humanae-vitae.html

Second Vatican Council's Decree on Ecumenism, *Unitatis Redintegratio*, 21 November 1964, https://www.vatican.va/archive/hist_councils/ii_vatican_council/documents/vat-ii_decree_19641121_unitatis-redintegratio_en.html

The Sacred Congregation for the Sacraments and Divine Worship document *Inaestimabile Donum*, dated 3 April 1980, https://www.papalencyclicals.net/jp02/inaestimabile-donum.htm

ABOUT THE AUTHORS

Fr. John Noone

John Noone was born in Ireland in December 1941. He grew up in Ireland with his family.

He was ordained on June 10, 1967 at St. Patrick's College, Carlow, Ireland and came to United States shortly after.

He received Master's Degree in Social Work from Tulane University in New Orleans in 1971 and became a citizen of the United States in 1972.

He received the following appointments: 1967-1970 Assistant Pastor of Our Lady of the Gulf, Bay St. Louis, MS; 1970 Assistant Director of Catholic Charities; 1977 Director of Catholic Social Services for the newly established Diocese of Biloxi, MS; 1983-2014 Pastor at churches in the Dioceses; 2014 Retired.

He continues working on his calling to get the truth out to all who are looking for it.

Fr. John Noone has compiled information for several CDs and books through the years of his priesthood from various sources and from his parishioners.

Ron Young

Ron Young, a convert to Catholicism and having a wealth of knowledge about the Bible and the Church, researched these subjects thoroughly.

ACKNOWLEDGMENTS

Special thanks to all parishioners who contributed to and made this book possible.
Formatting for POD and eBook by BookNook.biz
Cover design by BookNook.biz
Revisions and editing by Carolyn Seal, OFS

QUESTIONS INDEX

Sin

The Bible

God

Birth Control

The Papacy

Purgatory

Heaven

Mary

The Saints and Angels

The Rosary

Jesus

Practices

Sacramentals

History

Salvation/Justification

Charismatic Movement

The Sacraments

Baptism

Confirmation

Eucharist

Penance/Reconciliation/Confesion

Sacrament of the Sick

Holy Orders

Matrimony

Miscellaneous

Made in the USA
Coppell, TX
28 June 2026

83122511R00144